Risk Management

Concepts and Guidance

EDITED BY CARL L. PRITCHARD

Originally published by the
Defense Systems
Management College

Updated for the '90s by
ESI International

ESI International
Arlington, Virginia

Published by

ESI International
4301 N. Fairfax Drive
Arlington, Virginia 22203

Printed in the United States of America

ISBN 1-890367-06-0

Contents

Figures

Tables

Preface

Knowledge of risk management techniques is critically important to project team members and organizational leaders. Time and again, management must seek solutions to risk management issues. In the mid-1980s, the U.S. Department of Defense (DOD) sought such insight from the U.S. General Accounting Office (GAO). Thus in 1986, GAO developed an extensive report on risk management: *Technical Risk Assessment—The Status of Current DOD Efforts* (GAO 1986). In response to the GAO report, the Defense Systems Management College (DSMC) updated and expanded their 1983 *Risk Assessment Techniques Guide.*

From 1986 through the late 1990s, only a few guides to project risk management were written, and most lacked the depth of research developed for the 1986 GAO report. The requirement for a comprehensive risk book, coupled with the need for an update, prompted the development of this book, *Risk Management: Concepts and Guidance,* which is based on the DSMC risk management guide developed originally in the mid-1980s to provide support and guidance on U.S. government programs. It has been modified significantly to bring it into closer alignment with the management practices of the late 1990s and to make it more applicable to project managers outside the government.

In developing the original book, more than 380 surveys were sent out to more than 70 project offices and 25 contractors. The risk techniques resulting from this effort have not been evaluated for all circumstances; therefore, you must determine the validity and appropriateness of a particular technique for your own applications.

My heartfelt thanks go to the teams that contributed so diligently to this text as it was developed. I thank my fellow project managers and instructors at ESI International, who offered their time and attention to the review and development of this material. Thanks as well to the internal teams who made significant contributions as this publication was shepherded from word processing through editorial and, ultimately, to the print shop.

Special thanks go to Susan Deavours, Chester Zhivanos, and Kathy Richardson, talented editors whose guidance led to a major restructuring of the material to make it more accessible and clear. My thanks for their insight and candor in developing the text. Thanks to Barbara Raab for her innovation in creating the cover design. And finally, my heartfelt appreciation as well to Linda Nowak, our word processor, whose tireless efforts kept us on schedule as this text evolved.

About the Editor

Carl L. Pritchard is the Director of Distance Learning for ESI International and a widely recognized risk management instructor who presents programs around the world. Mr. Pritchard's publications include courses in risk management, as well as *Managing Projects in Organizations—The CD-ROM* with J. Davidson Frame. He is also a contributor to Dr. David Cleland's latest project management text, *A Field Guide to Project Management*.

In his role as a project management instructional designer and trainer, Mr. Pritchard analyzes, develops, and delivers training programs addressing project management tools, methods, skills, and competencies in courses such as *Risk Management; Scheduling and Cost Control; Project Management Applications; Managing Projects in Organizations; Innovation Project Management; The Winning Proposal; Project Planning, Analysis, and Control; Customer Relations; Project Management for Executives; Communications in Project Management; Writing and Presenting to Win;* and *Strategic Project Management*. In addition, he has developed guidebooks on using automated project management software tools and has worked with clients to assess their needs and objectives for project management. As a former major-market news director, he has considerable experience in researching and developing materials for the public.

Mr. Pritchard is active in professional project management associations and is a certified Project Management Professional (PMP*). He earned a B.A. in journalism from The Ohio State University.

Mr. Pritchard lives in Frederick, Maryland, with his wife, Nancy, and two sons, Adam and James.

---

*PMP is a registered Certification Mark of the Project Management Institute, Inc.

About ESI International

ESI International is a training and consulting firm founded as Educational Services Institute in 1981. For the past 15 years, our professionals have helped other professionals acquire knowledge and competencies in contract management, nonprofit and public administration management, global business management, and project management.

Our one-of-a-kind curriculum has become the world's premier professional development program in project management. Tens of thousands of professionals from around the world have benefited from seven core courses and dozens of electives leading to Master's Certificates in either Project Management or Information Technology Project Management from The George Washington University. In 1996 alone, we presented 1- to 5-day sessions to nearly 28,000 attendees on six continents. We also develop and teach tailored sessions as requested by many of the world's largest corporations in diverse industries, such as telecommunications, oil exploration and refining, financial services, and computer manufacturing.

ESI provides a variety of project management consulting services ranging from individual and organizational assessments, to methodology development, to hands-on coaching and mentoring.

Call 1-703-558-3020 for a catalog, or visit our Web site at http://www.esi-intl.com.

Introduction

Risk Management: Concepts and Guidance is designed to provide a fresh perspective on risk, built on a well-established background. As a reference volume, it provides a fundamental introduction on the basics associated with particular techniques. As an educational tool, it clarifies the concepts of risk and how they apply in projects.

When originally published, this material was geared (almost exclusively) to the government environment. In this version, the book also reflects commercial issues in the context of modern project terminology. In addition, the book aligns concepts and principles with the current version of *A Guide to the Project Management Body of Knowledge (PMBOK)*, produced by the Project Management Institute Standards Committee (1996).

Although there was no clear way to correlate these two documents perfectly, this book reflects the bulk of the terminology used in the PMBOK. The most significant departure comes in the phases of risk management. The Project Management Institute refers to risk identification, risk quantification, risk response development, and risk response control. This text analyzes an additional preliminary step called risk planning, which incorporates the broad-ranging issues associated with preparing project organizations with an infrastructure and strategies for risk.

Scope

Risk management is a "method of managing that concentrates on identifying and controlling the areas or events that have a potential of causing unwanted change . . . it is no more and no less than informed management" (Caver 1985). In keeping with this definition, this book covers project risk management from the project manager's perspective. It does not cover insurance risk, safety risk, or accident risk. Risk management, an integral part of project management, should be thought of as a project management *methodology*, rather than as an independent function distinct from other project management functions.

Approach

A holistic approach to risk is used in *Risk Management*. That is, risk is addressed as a single entity consisting of five facets: technical, programmatic, supportability, cost, and schedule. Although technical issues are a primary source of risk and figure prominently throughout the book, they must be balanced with managing other aspects of the project. Therefore, a fair amount of time is spent examining each facet of risk so that the interrelationships between the different facets can be understood.

Throughout the text, risk is considered exclusively as a future phenomenon. Risks are events that *may* happen to a project. They are not events that have already occurred. It is vital to consider risk in that context, because otherwise, every negative issue or change in plans may potentially be labeled as a risk event.

Using This Book

When using *Risk Management,* remember that risk is a complex concept subject to individual perception. Some people take risks, and some people are risk averse. Hence, it is difficult to develop universal rules for dealing with risk, but this book includes guidance, structure, and sample handling techniques that follow sound management practices. Although the principles, practices, and theories presented hold true in nearly all situations, under certain circumstances, the rules by which risk is evaluated may change drastically. For example, when confronted by an extreme threat, people can do extraordinary things. They will take risks that under ordinary circumstances would be deemed unacceptable. Hence, high-risk projects are not always bad and should not necessarily be avoided. Rather, if assumed, they should be rigorously monitored and controlled.

Risk Management is structured in a tutorial fashion and is presented in two parts. Part I begins by analyzing the systems that can be used to apply risk management (Chapter 1). The next chapter defines risk in terms relevant to project management and establishes the basic concepts necessary to understand the nature of risk. Then Chapter 3 defines the risk management structure and process that can be applied to all project phases.

Part II presents the specific techniques necessary to successfully carry out the processes described in Part I. Using these techniques, the project manager can gain some of the insights essential to proceed with risk management implementation. The techniques evaluated include analogy comparison, cost risk/WBS simulation model, decision analysis, estimating relationships, expert interviews, life-cycle cost analysis, network analysis, performance tracking, plan evaluation, project templates, risk factors, and three other common techniques occasionally used in support of risk management (but for which there are very limited data). The last chapter describes risk response control, the final step of putting the risk findings from the techniques into practice with your team and on your project. The Epilogue provides some modest insight on the future of risk management and what its practitioners can expect in the months and years to come.

The appendixes serve as reference materials and provide supporting detail for some of the concepts presented in the text:

- *Appendix A, Contractor Risk Management:* A review of some standard clauses and language incorporated to address contractor risk issues.

- *Appendix B, Abbreviated List of Risk Sources:* A compilation that serves as an initial risk checklist.

- *Appendix C, Basic Probability Concepts:* A refresher and basic primer for the material in the text.

- *Appendix D, Quantifying Expert Judgment:* How to transform qualitative information into quantitative information during expert interviews.

- *Appendix E, Special Notes on Software Risk:* A series of tables designed to support probability and impact analysis in software projects.

Risk Management also provides a glossary, bibliography, and index. The following table serves as a quick reference to locate critical subjects addressed in the text.

As you work through all this material, remember that risk is a highly personal and unique experience. No two projects will share exactly the same risks. As such, the ultimate authority on risk is not the tools and techniques addressed between these covers. The ultimate authority on any project's risk is the project manager: you!

Guide to Sections	Determining the need	Understanding risk	Planning for risk management	Organizing for risk management	Requiring contractor risk management	Risk identification	Risk quantification	Analyzing program risks	Communicating risk	Handling risk	Monitoring contractor risk management	Researching risk management	Tools	Probability theory
Organization (Introduction)			✓	✓										
Resources (Introduction)			✓			✓								
Communicating risk data (Introduction)			✓				✓	✓	✓					
Part I	✓													
Risk concepts (Ch. 2)		✓										✓		
Risk definition (Ch. 2)		✓										✓		
Risk facets and interrelationships (Ch. 2)		✓										✓		
Risk management perspectives (Ch. 2)		✓										✓		
Risk management structure (Ch. 3)			✓			✓	✓	✓		✓		✓		
Risk management planning (Ch. 3)			✓	✓			✓							
Risk assessment (Ch. 3)						✓	✓							
Risk response development (Ch. 3)								✓						
Risk response control (Ch. 3)										✓				
Executing risk management process (Part II)			✓			✓	✓	✓	✓	✓		✓	✓	
Assessment techniques (Part II)			✓			✓	✓						✓	
Analysis techniques (Part II)						✓	✓	✓					✓	
Handling techniques (Part II)										✓			✓	
Risk management implementation (Part II)			✓	✓	✓	✓						✓		
Technique selection (Ch. 16)			✓			✓		✓						
Contractor risk management (App. A)					✓						✓	✓		
Government responsibilities (App. A)					✓						✓	✓		
Contractor responsibilities (App. A)					✓						✓	✓		
Basic probability (App. C)		✓					✓							✓

RISK PROCESSES AND PRACTICES

RISK PROCESSES AND PRACTICES

The first part of *Risk Management: Concepts and Guidance* reviews the basic processes and practices associated with risk management in the project environment. It does so in depth, assessing the "rules of the road" in planning for, assessing, developing responses to, and controlling risk. It is a conceptual overview of how risk should be addressed.

In the development of this book's original source material, an extensive study was conducted to learn some of the best practices in risk management. The General Accounting Office (1986) report described five criteria considered essential in technical risk assessment. These criteria, which apply to more than just technical risks, are as follows:

- *Prospective analysis:* Possible future technical problems are considered, along with current problems.

- *Planned procedures:* An analysis is planned and systematic—not incidental.

- *Attending to technical risk:* Explicit attention is given to technical risk, not just to schedule or cost risk (consideration of technical risk is implicit).

- *Documentation:* Technical risk evaluation procedures and results are in written form.

- *Reevaluation at each phase:* New or updated evaluations are conducted to detect changes in risk during a system's development.

Without understanding the complexity of dealing with risk, these criteria appear to be merely reasonable. With an understanding of the complexity of risk, the importance of adhering to these criteria becomes evident. *Risk Management* will make you aware of how critical these criteria are and why they are mandatory for successful risk management.

Chapter 1

RISK MANAGEMENT PRACTICES

Most decisions, including simple ones, involve risk. Early in an effort, it is important to determine success criteria, the most important elements in a risk assessment. Consider, for example, the decision to drive or fly on a business trip. If cost is the only success criterion, risk determination is simple: compare the costs of flying and driving. But another success criterion might be safety, and thus statistics concerning accidents should be evaluated. If punctual arrival is added as a third criterion, airline on-time statistics, automobile dependability, and road conditions should be evaluated. As success criteria are added and made more complicated, decision making involves more judgment. In the example, increased cost is perhaps an acceptable risk, being late may be an unacceptable risk, and not arriving safely is certainly unacceptable.

Increasing technical complexity in today's projects increases risk. Decisions are biased heavily toward cost and schedule goals. Cost and schedule are understood, but the effect of cost and schedule decisions related to technical performance risk may not be as clear. Thus, a formal methodology to evaluate the effects of decision making and foreseeable problems is necessary. In addition, this methodology should help identify practical and effective workarounds to achieve project goals.

A Systematic Process

Not all projects require a formal risk management approach, but risk management must become a systematic process applied in a disciplined manner to obtain the maximum benefit. To ensure that the approach is systematic, the risk must be communicated, as perceived by each diverse technical function, to a single decision maker.

Although many project managers use intuitive reasoning (guessing) as the starting point in the decision-making process, the astute manager looks beyond reasoning and experience in making decisions that involve significant risks. At a minimum, the manager should ascertain the level of risk and the effect of the action on the progress of the project. If the risk is large enough to make the entire project fail, then it may not be acceptable, and some other plan or approach must be devised.

Several problems have prohibited risk management from becoming a clearly understood process. *Risk Management: Concepts and Guidance* addresses these problems and lays the groundwork for institutionalizing risk management. The structure used throughout the book (and defined in Chapter 3) is depicted in Figure 1. Note that risk management contains four specific elements. Risk planning incorporates all the tasks associated with building the organizational infrastructure to establish risk management as an element of project management. The remaining three steps refer to the actual implementation of the process.

All project managers should perform some documented risk management activity, either qualitative or quantitative. All significant projects should have formal, intense risk management activities; smaller, less critical projects may require less effort. The ultimate authority is the project manager, who must make the determination based on the project's cost, schedule, and performance challenges.

Summary

- Risk management is essential.
- Risk management should be systematic.
- All projects should have a documented risk management activity.

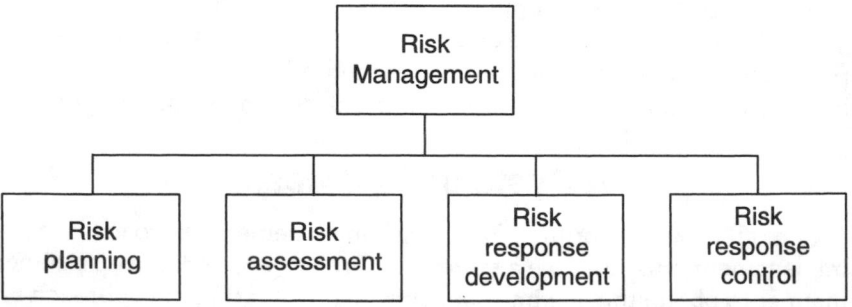

Figure 1. Risk Management Structure

Chapter 2

RISK CONCEPTS

Risk is defined as the probability of an undesirable event's occurring and the significance of the consequence of that occurrence (an event and its probability and impact). This differs from uncertainty, which considers only the likelihood of the occurrence of an event. (The traditional view defines risk as a situation in which an outcome is subject to an uncontrollable random event stemming from a known probability distribution. Although this definition has its place in statistics, it is of limited value in project risk management.) Although the terms *risk* and *uncertainty* are often used interchangeably, they are not the same.

To understand whether an event is truly "risky," the project manager must understand the potential effects resulting from its occurrence or nonoccurrence. Some judgment must be used in determining risk in this manner. For example, an event may have a low likelihood of occurring, but the consequences, if it does occur, can be catastrophic. A commercial flight exemplifies such a situation. The probability of a crash is low, but generally, the consequences are grave. Although many people feel uncomfortable about flying because of the consequences of failure, most people do not consider flying a high risk. This example also highlights that risk depends greatly on individual perception.

In using Figure 2 to assess risk, three factors are required. The first factor is the probability that the event will occur. Statistical data and probability theory play important roles in determining this variable. The second factor is the severity of the consequence if the event occurs. Again, statistics and probability help determine the degree of impact after it is identified. Note, however, that probability is of limited use here and is not always appropriate. The third factor required is subjective judgment based on the first and second factors.

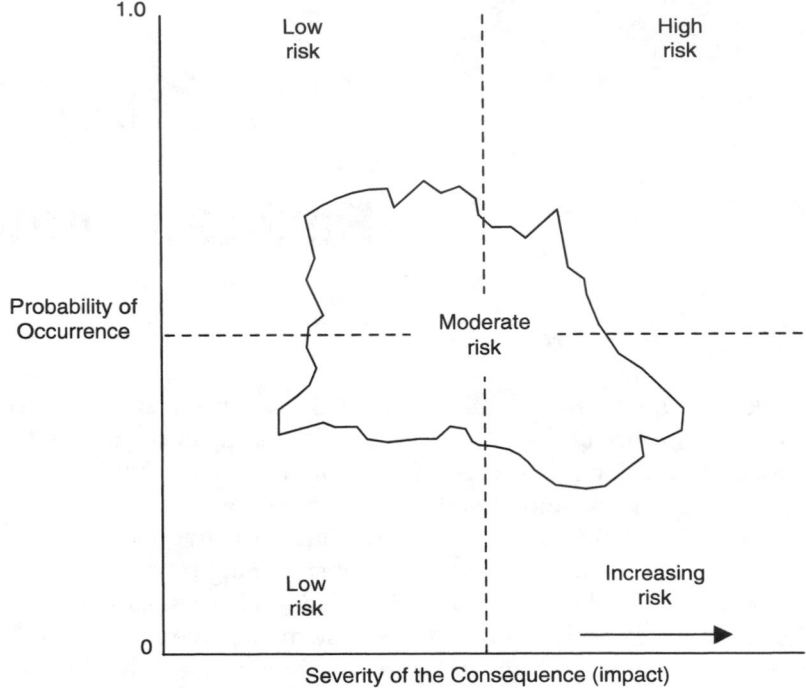

Figure 2. Concept of Risk

There can be little disagreement about the level of risk if the first two variables are as follows:

- Low probability and low impact equal low risk

- High probability and high impact equal high risk

- High probability and low impact equal low risk (to the project's overall success)

As you move toward the low probability/high impact quadrant of the figure, determining the risk level becomes more subjective and requires strict guidelines. A project with many moderate-risk items may be considered a high risk; a project with a few high-risk items may have a lower overall risk rating. These situations usually require some type of modeling to ascertain the project risk level. Many attempts have been made to model this subjective quantification of risk mathematically. Statisticians and some project managers may apply probability distributions (see Appendix C), others may not.

As stakeholders rate risks, disagreements can occur. Although project managers must sometimes rely on technical experts in the risk management process, they must also be prepared to make the final judgment themselves. Some guidelines on rating risks are included in Chapter 3 under "Risk Quantification." And although it is important to look at the quantifiable probabilities for loss, another item to consider is opportunity. If no real opportunity exists, there is no reason to pursue a risky activity. However, as the potential gain increases, so does the threshold for accepting risk.

Classifying Risk into Facets

All projects that are planned properly will provide the project manager with some reserve funds and slack time to work around unanticipated problems and still meet original cost, schedule, and performance goals. But a wide variety of problems can keep the manager from meeting project objectives. To the project manager, risks are all rooted in the process to deliver a specified product or service at a specified time for a specified cost. Each aspect has a potential risk of failure: the product may not attain the performance level specified, the actual costs may be too high, or delivery may be too late. (There is, of course, a risk that the original cost, schedule, and performance goals were unattainable, unrealistic, or conflicting.)

Risk must be classified to make it manageable. Five facets of risk are used to manage cost, schedule, and performance issues faced on a project:

- Technical (performance related)
- Programmatic (performance related)
- Supportability (environment related)
- Cost
- Schedule

Because they are (more or less) indicators of project status, cost and schedule risks are treated somewhat differently from the others. However, cost and schedule can become a major source of project risk. Sample risks from each facet are shown in Table 1.

Classifying a risk into one or more of the five facets requires examining the source of the risk. It is not always easy to determine the appropriate category, and just for the sake of classification, it is not that

Table 1. Typical Sources of Risk by Facet

Risk Facet	Sources of Risk	
Technical	Physical properties	Requirement changes
	Material properties	Fault detection
	Radiation properties	Operating environment
	Testing and modeling	Proven or unproven technology
	Integration and interface	
	Software design	System complexity
	Safety	Unique or special resources
Programmatic	Material availability	Labor strikes
	Personnel availability	Requirement changes
	Personnel skills	Political advocacy
	Safety	Contractor stability
	Security	Funding profile
	Environmental impact	Regulatory changes
	Communication problems	
Supportability	Reliability and maintainability	Facility considerations
	Training and training support	Interoperability considerations
	Equipment	Transportability
	Human resource considerations	Computer resources support
	System safety	Packaging, handling, storage
	Technical data	
Cost	Sensitivity to technical risk	Sensitivity to schedule risk
	Sensitivity to programmatic risk	Overhead and general and administrative rates
	Sensitivity to supportability risk	Estimating error
Schedule	Sensitivity to technical risk	Sensitivity to cost risk
	Sensitivity to programmatic risk	Degree of concurrency
		Number of critical path items
	Sensitivity to supportability risk	Estimating error

important. However, understanding the source of the risk and the affected areas, as well as providing a structure to examine risk, are critical elements if the risk is to be managed effectively.

Technical Risk

Technical risk is the risk associated with evolving a new design (or approach) either to provide a greater level of performance or to accommodate some new constraints. The nature and causes of technical risks are as varied as approaches and system designs. Many, if not most, technical risks result from the omnipresent requirement to minimize or maximize physical properties of processes, systems, and equipment. What is technically risky at first may become routine later; risky areas on a project with high performance requirements may be routine on systems with lower performance requirements.

Many of the "-ilities," such as reliability, maintainability, and long-term viability, must be addressed in the project environment. All can be viewed as additional requirements placed on system or process designers attempting to evolve an efficient design capable of the desired performance level. And all can be a source of risk.

Describing all possible technical risks is not easy, because when examined at the lowest level of detail, there are so many. Usually, many items or steps are to be designed and integrated with other items and steps. There may be several design objectives for each site, and each combination of item and design objective is subject to many "-ility" requirements as well as cost and schedule constraints. Appendix B contains an abbreviated list of technical risk areas. It does not list types of risks by processes, components, parts, subassemblies, assemblies, subsystems, and systems for all the many associated integration design tasks. Nor does it address all possible aspects of performance, which vary widely from project to project. As the design architecture, performance, and other requirements and project constraints become known on a given project, a more detailed list of risks should be prepared based on project-specific information.

Programmatic Risk

Programmatic risk is the risk associated with obtaining and using applicable resources and activities that can affect project direction but that may be outside the project manager's control. Generally, programmatic risks are not directly related to improving the state of the art.

Programmatic risks are grouped into categories based on the nature and source of factors that have the potential to disrupt the project's implementation plan:

- Disruptions caused by decisions made at higher levels of authority directly related to the project

- Disruptions caused by events or actions affecting the project but not directed specifically at it

- Disruptions caused primarily by a failure to foresee production-related problems

- Disruptions caused by imperfect capabilities

- Disruptions caused primarily by a failure to foresee problems other than those included in the first four categories

These risks tend to be a function of the business environment. Appendix B has a more detailed listing of sample programmatic risks.

Supportability Risk

Supportability risk is the risk associated with fielding and maintaining systems or processes that are currently being developed or that have been developed and are being deployed. Supportability risk comprises both technical and programmatic aspects. Certainly, any design effort (which may contain technical challenges) should consider what the supportability issues are likely to be when the system is fielded. Another example is training, which is generally a programmatic risk but quickly becomes a supportability risk when maintenance and operations support become the main factors.

It is important to understand that any given risk area may belong to more than one of the five facets cited earlier. For example, a particular piece of support equipment may pose a technical challenge *and* have significant supportability implications.

Cost and Schedule Risk

A long history of project cost and schedule growth is present in many organizations. In a time of limited budgets, cost and schedule growth in one project may dictate reductions in another. Therefore, the risk of cost and schedule growth is a major concern. This problem is further complicated because performance and design technical problems are sometimes solved by increasing the planned project scope, thereby increasing project cost and/or schedule.

Cost and schedule growth is the difference between the estimated project cost and schedule and the actual cost and schedule. Therefore, two major risk areas have an effect on cost and schedule growth:

- Unreasonably low cost or schedule estimates

- A project not carried out efficiently enough to meet reasonable cost or schedule objectives

The outcome of the second of these two risk areas is not primarily a cost or schedule *analysis*-related risk. Cost, schedule, or financial analyses will have little influence over the outcome. The final costs and schedules are primarily a function of the skill of the project manager in accommodating unanticipated problems related to technical, programmatic, and supportability risks. The lack of a good solution for such problems often increases costs and schedules.

An unrealistically low baseline cost or schedule estimate can result from any of four categories (before a pricing decision):

- Inadequate system description

- Inadequate historical cost or schedule database

- Lack of sound methods relating historical costs and schedules to new project costs

- Incomplete cost or schedule estimate

Note that from this context, there are few true cost or schedule risks. More often than not, cost or schedule uncertainty reflects technical, programmatic, and supportability risk.

Facet Organization

There are risk drivers and risk indicators. Risk drivers are usually the technical, programmatic, and supportability facets; cost and schedule facets are the indicators. Generally for contract items, a specified performance level must be met. This includes design criteria, supportability factors, performance criteria, and a host of other specifics. The next question is what will it take to perform this activity in terms of resources (time and money). That the activity satisfies the need is paramount. The tendency then is to focus on the performance requirements—not on cost or schedule. Unfortunately, cost and schedule tend to be the yardsticks by which decisions are made, and the trade-offs among cost, schedule, and performance are not well understood.

This is one of the advantages of performing risk management. It attempts to draw reality into the relationship between the risk facets. A project is sometimes undertaken with the understanding that the resulting product will be the best possible within the monetary and time constraints dictated. In these cases, the cost and schedule facets become the drivers and the other facets may become the indicators.

But few projects have such clear-cut goals. More often than not, the project manager must strive to achieve a balance between the facets to reach seemingly conflicting goals in cost, schedule, and performance. For simplicity, this book treats technical, programmatic, and support-ability risks as the predominant factors affecting cost and schedule risks, as illustrated in Figure 3.

By now it is clear that the risk facets are not independent of one another. Although a design risk is technical in nature, it may have cost

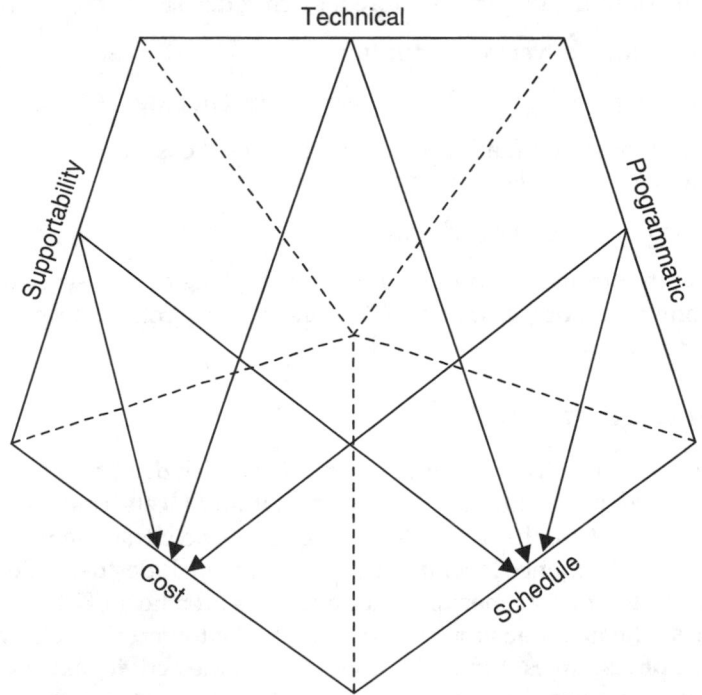

Figure 3. Relationships Among the Five Risk Facets

or schedule impacts. Or a tight test window that presents a schedule risk may also have serious technical impacts. The facets may also change with time. What started as a technical risk in the design of a product may surface years later as a supportability risk factor that has serious cost and schedule impacts. A useful approach is to examine all facets whenever a risk is identified in one facet.

This discussion does not imply that cost and schedule manage themselves—that is certainly not true. The intent is to emphasize the importance of managing the *source* of the risk in any project. Frequently, this is some factor rooted in technical, programmatic, or supportability characteristics.

Other Relevant Considerations

Two other areas are worthy of mention when discussing risk concepts in terms of projects. Both deal with organizational management structure.

Two Perspectives of Risk Management

Project risk management must be viewed from two vantage points:

- *Short-term perspective:* Dealing with the current project phase and the immediate future

- *Long-term perspective:* Dealing with anything beyond the short term

Like many other aspects of risk management, the distinction between the two perspectives is somewhat unclear, and further explanation is needed to define and justify the separation. The short-term perspective normally refers to managing risk related to satisfying the immediate needs of the project: "This is the performance level I need to achieve today, and how are my contractors managing to achieve this?" The long-term perspective deals with "What can I do today to ensure that the project, in the end, will be a success?" This might include, among other things, introducing engineering issues related to project support and production into the design process earlier in the project.

The short- and long-term perspectives are closely linked. In achieving the desired performance level in the short term, the project manager may be forced to sacrifice long-term capability. Projects that require new approaches or new tools may suffer in the short term but have higher productivity and performance levels in the long term. As with any good management decisions, the short-term and long-term implications must be well understood. The project manager provides a risk response early only if these implications are known.

Another look at the two perspectives is illustrated in Figure 4, which depicts an overall design selected for a project that has certain elements of risk. This was a decision that obviously had long-term implications. The current task for the project manager is to complete this design within the existing resource constraints. The project manager has selected some technical, cost, and schedule parameters to manage risk on an operational, day-to-day basis (short-term risk management). While focusing on the short term, the project manager must also keep an eye on long-term implications.

Realities of Project Management

Ideally, the same management team would stay with a project from the earliest phases through closeout. However, ideal conditions rarely exist, and a given project will likely see several management and staff teams. The transition in project management personnel often creates voids in the risk management process. These voids create knowledge gaps, losing valuable information from earlier in the project. Precious time must be spent becoming familiar with the project—often at the sacrifice of long-term planning and risk management. A formal system for recording, analyzing, and acting on project risk facilitates the transition process and, when done properly, forces long-term risk management. The approach to formal risk management is contained in Chapter 3.

Although it is desirable to make decisions based on long-term implications, it is not always feasible. The project manager is often forced to act on short-term considerations. One reason for this has already been mentioned: the change in personnel. Another reason is project advocacy. Sudden shifts in organizational priorities can wreak havoc on long-term plans (a risk area in itself). This results in short-term actions to adjust to new priorities. Often these decisions are made before long-term effects can be evaluated thoroughly. Last, in some instances, long-term effects are not always apparent at the time a decision must be made.

Day-to-day operational risks must be addressed to complete any given phase of a project. As much as possible, the solutions developed

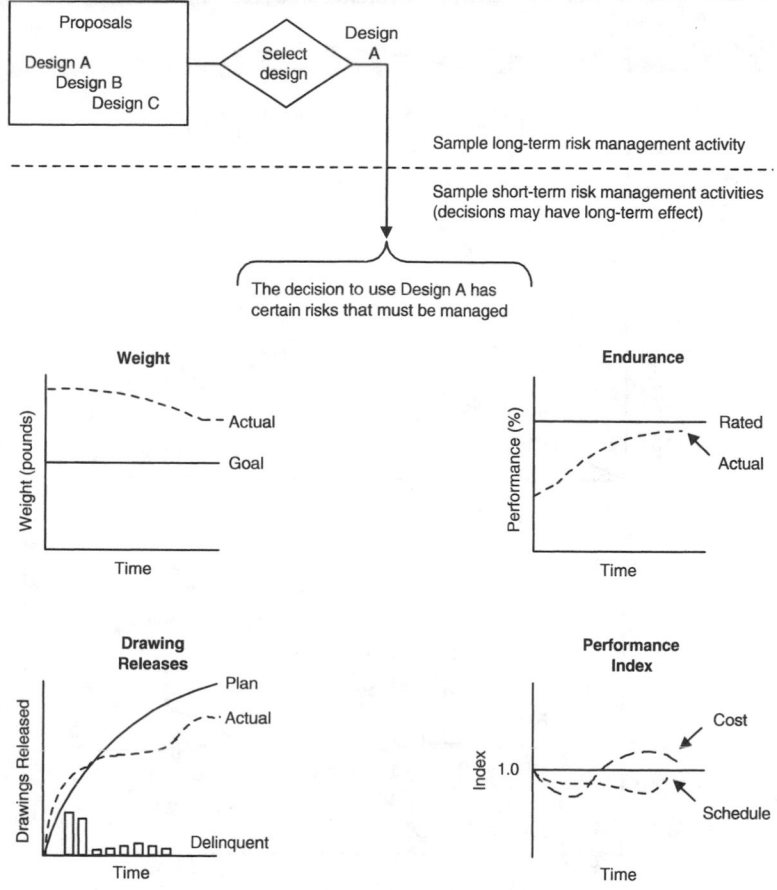

Figure 4. Short-Term and Long-Term Risk Perspectives

to handle these risks must be examined from a long-term viewpoint and must provide the project manager a strong, structured argument to defend his or her position. As many studies have pointed out, actions taken early in a project's development have a major effect on the overall performance and cost over the life of the project. One example is illustrated in Figure 5 (DSMC 1985).

Summary

- Risk considers both probability and impact.
- Rating risk is a subjective process requiring strict guidelines.

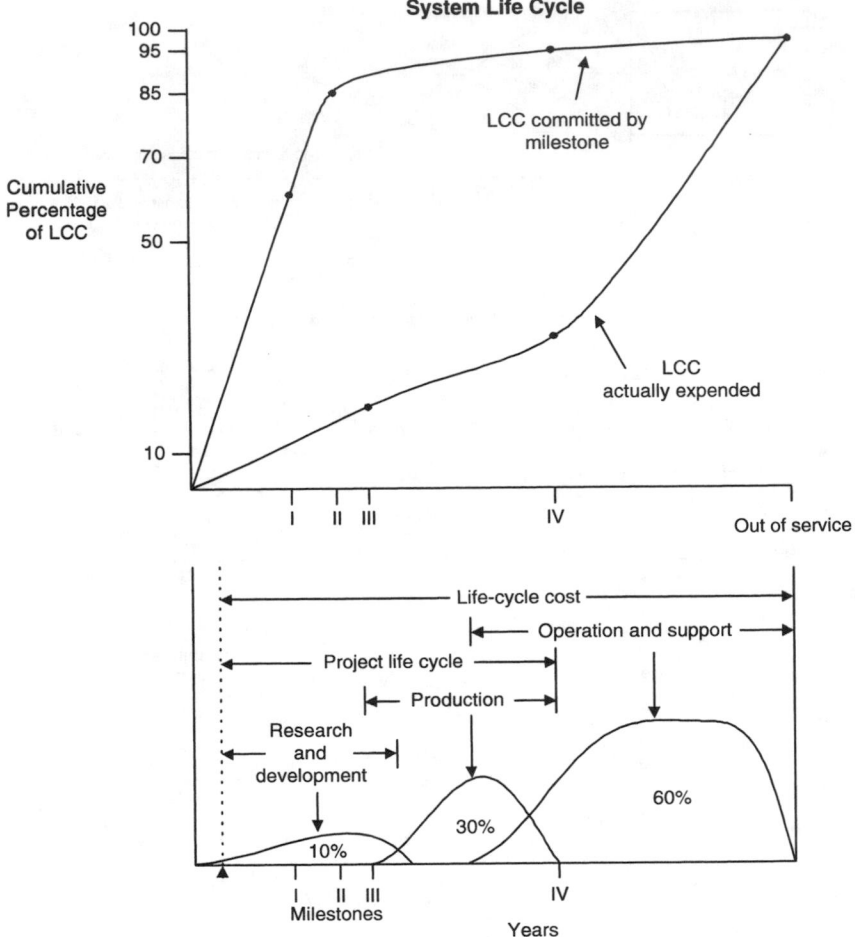

Figure 5. Life-Cycle Cost

- There are five facets to risk: technical, programmatic, support-ability, cost, and schedule.

- The risk facets are strongly interrelated.

- Most risk sources evolve from technical, programmatic, or supportability factors.

- Risk has both long-term and short-term perspectives.

Chapter 3

THE RISK MANAGEMENT STRUCTURE

This chapter focuses on defining and explaining the elements of risk management and presents the recommended overall structure for implementing risk management. In the past, several different structures and definitions have been used for basically the same concept, which has been a source of continuing confusion. Figure 6 illustrates both a time-tested structure that incorporates (but does not mirror) the perspective of the Project Management Institute's *A Guide to the Project Management Body of Knowledge* (1996) and an emphasis on planning and structure for capturing risk data.

Risk Planning

Risk, which is present in some form and to some degree in most human activity, is characterized by the following:

- Is usually at least partially unknown
- Changes with time
- Is manageable in the sense that human action may be applied to change its form and degree of effect

The purpose of risk planning is simply to compel project managers to give organized, purposeful thought to achieve the following:

- Isolate and minimize risk
- Eliminate risk wherever possible
- Develop alternative courses of action

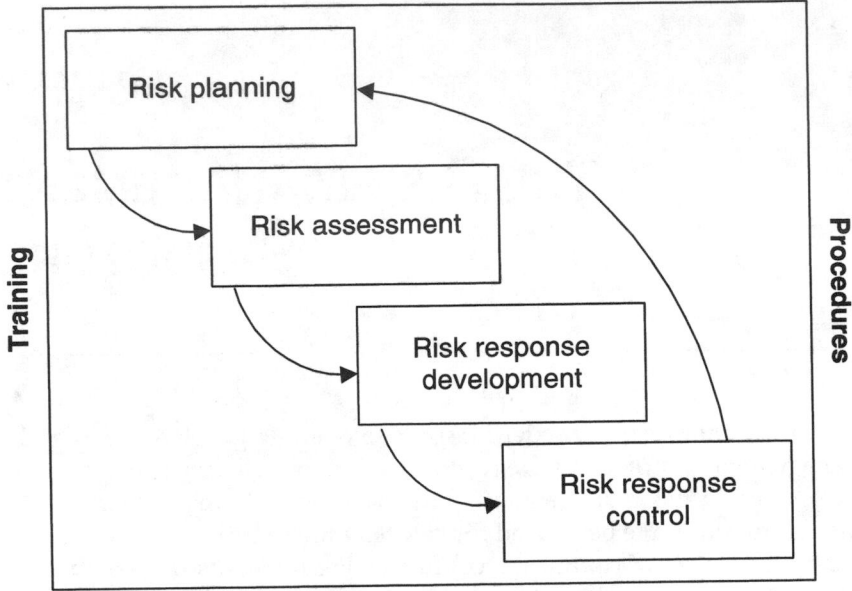

Figure 6. Risk Management Process

- Establish time and money reserves to cover risks that cannot be mitigated

Risk planning is sensibly done and redone as an integral part of normal project planning and management. It should occur at regular intervals. Some of the more obvious times for evaluating the risk management plan include the following:

- In preparation for major decision points
- In preparation for and immediately following evaluations
- Concurrent with reviewing and updating other project plans and specifications

Most major projects are guided by a series of plans that provide the rationale and intended processes through which projects will be executed. A risk management plan is recommended as part of this suite of guiding documents. Such a plan would publish the results or latest status of the risk management planning process.

Risk planning has not been developed as much as some other plans in terms of content and format, which allows project managers some latitude to establish documents that suit their situation. One approach to the content of a risk management plan is illustrated in Figure 7; the highlights are described in the following paragraphs.

- *System description and project summary:* This material should be the same in all the project's plans. It should provide the frame of reference for understanding the operational need, the mission, and the major functions of the project. It should include key operational and technical characteristics of the project deliverables, a project summary that includes a description of the organizational relationships and responsibilities of the participating organizations, and an integrated project schedule.

- *Approach to risk management:* This section includes the intended approach (from an organizational perspective) for executing the risk management elements (risk assessment, risk response development, and risk response control). Other appropriate items include the definitions, measurement techniques, and risk rating methods for the five risk facets (technical, programmatic, supportability, schedule, and cost).

- *Application issues and problems:* This section includes the procedures and processes for the following (at the project level):
  - Risk assessment
    - Risk identification
    - Risk quantification
    - Risk prioritization
  - Risk response development
  - Risk response control
    - Control evaluation
    - Risk documentation

- *Other relevant plans:* Every major project should be governed by a set of plans, including the project plan. Other plans may include quality, communication, contracting, testing, and training. Typically, these plans are not written from a risk viewpoint. But when read with risk in mind, they provide valuable information and may suggest items of risk. These plans should be reviewed before, during, and after preparing the risk management plan. The risk management plan may also suggest items to be addressed in the other plans. Although the risk management plan deals with

Part I, Description
    1.1   Objective
    1.2   Project
        1.2.1   Project description
        1.2.2   Key functions
    1.3   Required operational characteristics
    1.4   Required technical characteristics

Part II, Project Summary
    2.1   Summary requirements
    2.2   Management
    2.3   Integrated schedule

Part III, Approach to Risk Management
    3.1   Definitions
        3.1.1   Technical risk
        3.1.2   Programmatic risk
        3.1.3   Supportability risk
        3.1.4   Cost risk
        3.1.5   Schedule risk
    3.2   Structure
    3.3   Methods overview
        3.3.1   Techniques applied
        3.3.2   Implementation

Part IV, Application
    4.1   Risk assessment
        4.1.1   Risk identification
        4.1.2   Risk quantification
        4.1.3   Risk prioritization
    4.2   Risk response development
    4.3   Risk response control
        4.3.1   Control evaluation
        4.3.2   Risk documentation

Part V, Other Relevant Plans

Part VI, Summary
    6.1   Risk process summary
    6.2   Technical risk summary
    6.3   Programmatic risk summary
    6.4   Supportability risk summary
    6.5   Cost risk summary
    6.6   Schedule risk summary
    6.7   Conclusions

Part VII, Bibliography

Part VIII, Approval

Figure 7. Sample Risk Management Plan

analyzing and managing risk, risk should be identified and high-
lighted in any plan as appropriate.

Risk Assessment

Risk Identification

Risk identification is an organized, thorough approach to finding real
risks associated with a project. It is not a process of inventing highly
improbable scenarios in an effort to cover every conceivable possibility.
It is a critical step in the risk management process. Risks cannot be
assessed or managed until they are identified and described in an
understandable way.

- *Approaches:* Expert interviews, analogy comparisons, and the
  evaluation of project plans and strategies are especially useful
  techniques in risk identification. The objective is to obtain straightforward, clear narrative statements describing project risks.
  Mathematical techniques are not appropriate here. Part II details
  the techniques for analyzing risk.

- *Checklist concept:* The purpose of any project is to achieve a
  specified set of goals. The project must be scrutinized systematically to identify those events that may reasonably occur and
  threaten project goals. The search should emphasize "show-
  stoppers," those events that will have a major effect on the project.

  The top-level risk matrix (Table 2) is a tool designed to organize
  this process. It is applied at the total project level as a starting
  point. The concept can be refined and carried to greater detail as
  needed.

- *Defining project goals:* This would seem to be an easy task.
  However, because different stakeholders have different perspectives, it will be a thought-provoking and controversial process.
  Requirements specified in the project charter should be included
  as goals. If direction is missing or not explicit enough to be included as a goal, this process identifies that fact, which in itself is
  an important risk reduction action. Any "Goals" block that cannot
  be filled out to the project manager's satisfaction is an alert for
  direction or definition.

- *Defining project strategies:* Project strategies represent the plans for
  achieving the goals. Ideally, the "Strategy" blocks in the matrix

Table 2. Top-Level Risk Matrix

Risk Facet	Project Phase			
	Concept	Development	Implementation	Closeout
Technical Goals				
Strategy				
Risks				
Programmatic Goals				
Strategy				
Risks				
Supportability Goals				
Strategy				
Risks				
Schedule Goals				
Strategy				
Risks				
Cost Goals				
Strategy				
Risks				

should contain references to chapters or paragraphs in one or more of the project plans. If this is not the case, the plans are inadequate. This causes the greatest risk of all—not having a plan to reach a goal. The top-level risk matrix can serve as an incentive to ensuring that the plans address all goals.

- *Identifying risks:* A simple first step in risk identification is to evaluate whether organizational strategies are appropriate to the goals. Counterproductive strategies (passed down from higher management) cause risk. The imperfect world of organizational management frequently forces the project manager to do things that are counterproductive or less than optimal. Highlighting these anomalies contributes significantly to risk identification. Organizing and stratifying the identified risks is beneficial. Preliminary quantification is intended to begin ranking risks for further evaluation. Heavy mathematical treatment is *not* desired at this point.

Risk Quantification

Preliminary Quantification

The identification process produces a well-documented description of project risks. Before analysis begins in earnest, it helps to organize and stratify the identified risks. Preliminary quantification ranks risks for further evaluation.

- *Baselining risk:* Risk exists only in relation to the two absolute states of uncertainty: total failure (usually expressed as 0 percent probability) and total success (usually expressed as 100 percent probability). Risk will always fall somewhere within this range. The risk assessment process attempts to treat risk in relation to its probabilities. The process is simplified significantly by defining total failure and total success so that the full range of possibilities can be understood. Defining one or both of the baselines (cost and schedule) helps set a benchmark on the curves (Figure 8). It is certainly desirable (but difficult) to describe the technical content as an absolute percentage of 0 percent or 100 percent. Because most technical issues are tied to cost and schedule, those values can be applied with the assumption that technical content has been addressed. After defining a baseline position, it becomes easier to quantify the degree of risk for each impact area.

- *Rating schemes and definitions:* The degree of risk assigned in a given situation reflects the personality of the risk analyst. Twenty people can look at the same situation and each come up with a different risk value. A risk rating scheme built against an agreed-to set of definitions helps minimize the discrepancies.

  The rating system can (and probably should) be simple—such as high, medium, low—applying the notion that the degree of risk is a consideration of probability of occurrence and severity of impact. Figure 9 is a diagram for a risk rating mechanism. Defining a risk becomes a matter of identifying impacts, deciding on a scale, and then shaping the boundaries. With a defined risk rating scheme in place (at least tentatively), the task of evaluating and quantifying each identified risk may be accomplished using this structure.

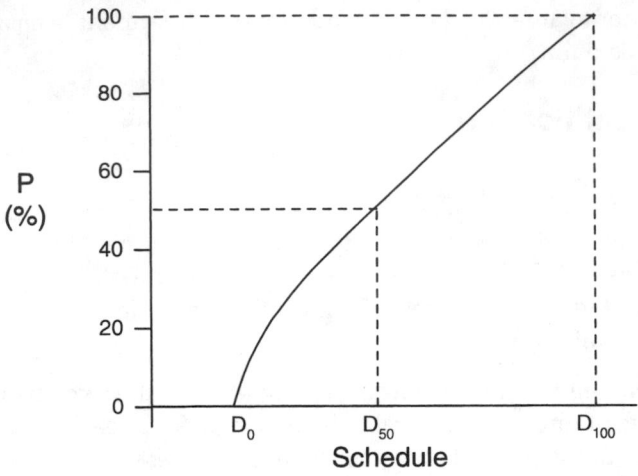

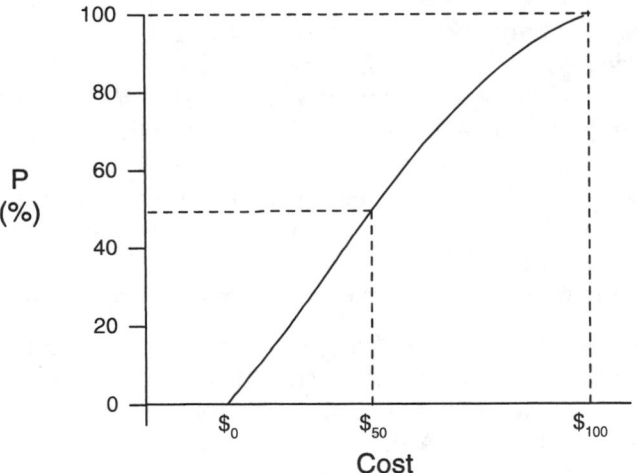

Figure 8. Risk Baselines

- *Interviewing experts:* The technique for interviewing technical experts to rate risk is discussed in detail in Chapter 4.

- *Using analogies:* Analogy comparison is an attempt to learn from other projects or situations and is used for many actions, such as cost estimating and scheduling. It is important to differentiate between analogous projects and projects with analogous risks. Analogy comparison is discussed in detail in Chapter 5.

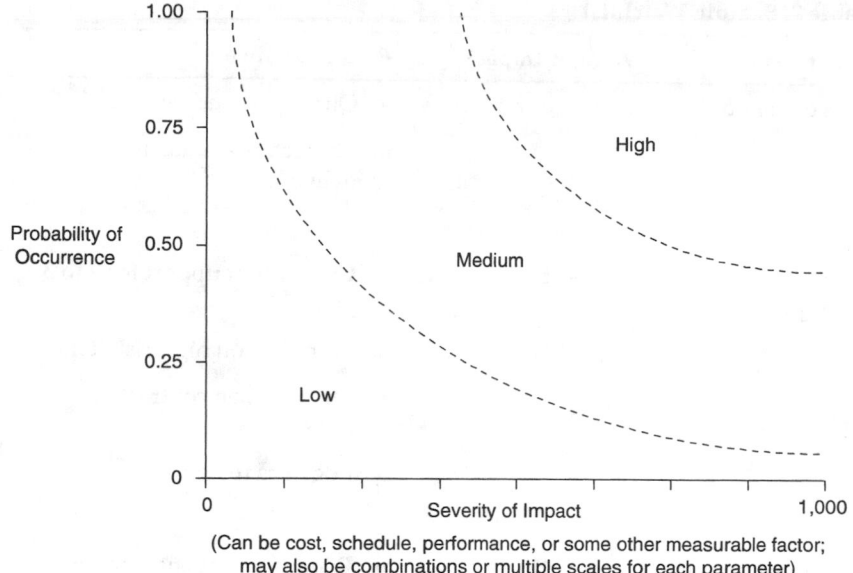

(Can be cost, schedule, performance, or some other measurable factor;
may also be combinations or multiple scales for each parameter)

Figure 9. Risk Rating

Detailed Risk Quantification

As time progresses in a risk management effort, the quantification function becomes independent from the identification function. Rather than analyzing risk at the smallest level, the process begins to focus on risk to the project as a whole. Risk quantification examines the effects of changes in impact *and* probability. A what-if analysis is an example of the activities that should take place during more detailed risk quantification.

Products of Risk Quantification

One of the most useful products of the analysis process is the watchlist, which is a list of the high-priority risks, as determined through risk quantification. The watchlist serves as the worksheet that managers use for recording risk management progress (Caver 1985). An example of a watchlist is shown in Table 3. Watchlists provide a convenient form to track and document output from the risk analysis process.

Cumulative probability distribution, another useful product of risk analysis, is illustrated in Figure 10. The cumulative probability

Table 3. Sample Watchlist

Event Item	Area of Impact	Risk Response
Loss of vendor	Production cost	<ul><li>Qualify second vendor</li><li>Get technical data as a deliverable</li></ul>
Incomplete logistic support analysis	Support cost	<ul><li>Contractor support for 2 to 3 years</li><li>Warranty on high-risk items</li><li>Emphasis on contractor reviews</li><li>Logistics reviews</li></ul>
Immature technical data package with many engineering changes for design fixes	Production cost with high first-unit cost	<ul><li>Require production engineers on contractor design team</li><li>Fixed-price contract</li><li>Competition</li><li>Producibility engineering planning</li><li>Production readiness reviews</li></ul>
Long lead-time items delayed	Production schedule	<ul><li>Get early identification of long lead-time items</li><li>Emphasis on early delivery</li><li>Transfer or leveling from less urgent programs</li></ul>

distribution curve is a common, conventional method used to portray cost, schedule, and performance risk. Project managers can use cumulative probability distributions by determining an appropriate risk level (threshold) for the item and then reading from the curve the corresponding target cost, schedule, or performance. This is a typical output of many automated risk tools. Appendix C explains probability curves in more detail.

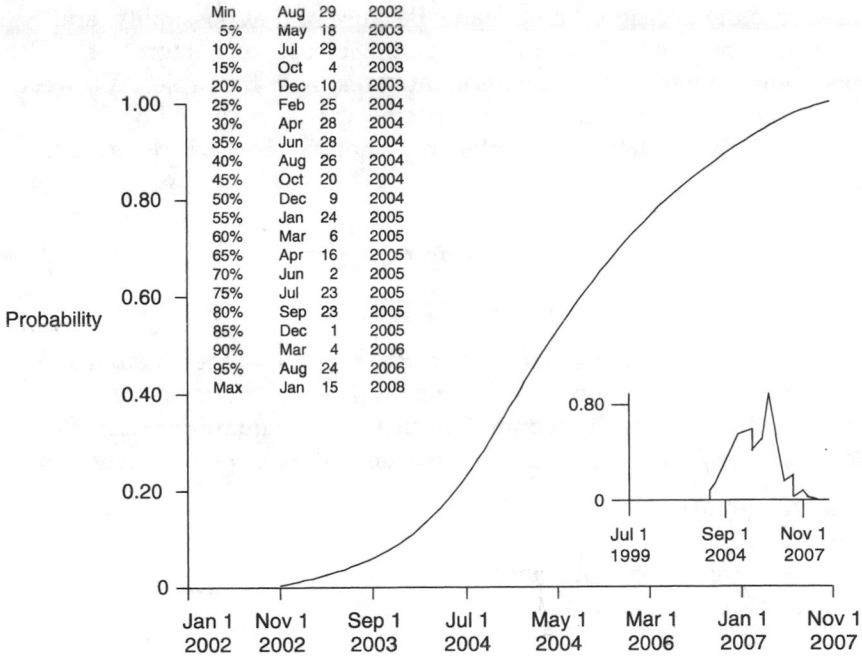

Figure 10. Sample Cumulative Probability Distribution

Risk analysis generally provides an in-depth understanding of the sources and degree of risk and can be portrayed quickly in a few charts. This generates an effective communication of project status to decision makers. Chapter 16 has suggestions for communicating risk information.

Risk Prioritization

After risks are quantified, the final step in the process is relatively simple. Risk prioritization involves the fundamental practice of ordering risks according to those that have the greatest potential to do harm to the project, the team, or the organization. Although the practice relies heavily on the products of risk quantification, it still involves some subjective judgments by the project manager. Specifically, the project manager must discern which risks have the greatest need for immediate attention, without waiting until it is too late to relegate vital decisions.

In many organizations, the project manager relies on the skills and judgments of experts to handle the prioritization. However, the risks inherent in that practice are that the "experts" may infuse their own biases into the decisions being made. Because of that possibility, and because of the reality that all risks involve at least some degree of uncertainty, the final determination must rest with the project manager. When it comes to prioritization, the project manager should be the ultimate decision maker in establishing what the most worrisome risks are.

Risk Response Development

Risk response development is a critical element in the risk management process that determines what action (if any) will be taken to address risk issues evaluated in identification and quantification efforts. Generally, response strategies fall into one of the following categories:

- Avoidance
- Control
  - Minimizing probability
  - Minimizing impact
  - Deflection
- Retention

Risk Avoidance

In many situations, a lower risk choice is available from a range of risk alternatives. Selecting a lower risk option represents a risk avoidance decision ("I accept this other option because of less potentially unfavorable results"). Certainly, not all risk should be avoided. On occasion, a higher risk can be deemed more appropriate because of design flexibility, enhanced performance, or the capacity for expansion.

Risk Control

Risk control is the most common of all the risk-handling strategies. It is the process of taking specific courses of action to reduce the probability, reduce the impact, or deflect the risk to another party. This often involves using reviews, risk reduction milestones, development of fallback positions, and similar management actions. The project manager must develop risk reduction plans and then track activities based on those plans. All these actions are built into the project plans (cost plans, schedule plans) and ultimately into the work breakdown structure (WBS).

Through risk control, the project manager may emphasize minimizing the probability that the risk will occur or minimizing the impact *if* the risk occurs. Depending on the specific risk, either approach may be effective.

Another way to control risk is to deflect it. When considering deflection, project managers may reduce risk exposure by sharing risk with customers and contractors. Risk deflection often benefits both the project and the customer. The type of contract, performance incentives, and warranties may be structured to share risk with others (and, in part, deflect risk).

Risk Retention

Risk retention is a decision to accept the consequences if the event occurs. Projects inherently involve retention of some risk. The project manager must determine what level of risk can be safely assumed in each situation as it evolves.

Risk Response Control

After risks are identified and quantified, and clear responses developed, those responses must be put into action. Risk response control is the daily active management of risk. It takes place as the project progresses. Risk response control involves implementing the risk management plan, which should be an integral part of the project plan.

The challenge is dealing with risk events as they occur. Flaws in carefully structured plans become evident when those plans are implemented. Some strategies work very effectively; others prove far less effective. Thus, it often becomes necessary to begin the cycle anew, which involves either reconsidering risk responses or migrating even further back in the process to reevaluate identified risks.

Summary

- Risk identification is the process of identifying project risks.

- Risk quantification is the process of quantifying risks against a well-defined rating scheme and honing that quantification to assess overall project impact.

- Risk response development involves evaluating and refining risk mitigation strategies.

- Risk response control is the implementation of those strategies.

- Risk management is a continual process throughout the project.

RISK MANAGEMENT TECHNIQUES

RISK MANAGEMENT TECHNIQUES

The second major part of this book introduces specific techniques that have proven useful to both customers and project managers in carrying out the risk management process.

Each chapter describes the techniques for accomplishing the basic steps of the risk management process: risk planning, risk assessment (identification, quantification, and prioritization), risk response development, and risk response control. Many of the techniques can serve more than one step of the process. For example, an in-depth evaluation of a critical path network is useful in initial overview evaluation, risk identification, and risk response development. The resource requirements, applications, and output capabilities of each of the techniques are summarized in Table 4. Multiple applications are listed in Table 5, with predominant use represented by solid circles and secondary applications by open circles.

In addition, each technique must be evaluated in context with consistent criteria to evaluate whether or not it is the most effective technique to apply. Those criteria include the following:

- Technique description
- When applicable
- Input and output
- Major steps in applying the technique
- Use of results
- Resource requirements
- Reliability
- Selection criteria

Table 4. Risk Analysis Technique Selection Matrix

Techniques	Resource Requirements					Applications							Output		
	Cost (resource-months)	Proper facilities and equipment	Implementation time (months)	Ease of use	Time commitment	Project status reporting	Major planning decisions	Contract strategy selection	Milestone preparation	Design guidance	Source selection	Budget submittal	Accuracy	Level of detail	Utility
Analogy comparisons	0.2–2	Y	0.2–2	M	S	L	H	H	L–M	M	H	L–M	L–M	L–H	M
Cost risk/WBS simulation model	0.2–0.4	N	0.2–0.5	E	M	L	H	NA	NA	M	L	L	L	L	L
Decision analysis	0.5–1	Y	0.2–0.6	M	S–M	M	H	H	M	M	M	M	L–H	L–H	M
Estimating relationships	0.1–3	Y	0.1–3	E	M	L	L	L	NA	NA	NA	H	L	L	L
Expert interviews	0.1–3	Y	0.1–3	E	S	H	H	M	H	M	H	L	L–H	M	H
Life-cycle cost analysis	0.5–3	Y	0.5–5	E	M	L–H	H	H	L	H	H	H	M	M	H
Network analysis	1–3	Y	1–3	D	S–M	H	H	M	H	M	H	L	H	L–H	H
Performance tracking	1.5	Y	1.5	E–M	M	H	H	M	M	H	M	M	M	M	H
Plan evaluation	1–1.5	Y	0.2–1.5	M	H	H	H	NA	L	M	L	L	H	H	M–H
Project templates	0.5	Y	0.5	E	M	H	H	H	H	H	M–H	L	M	L–H	H
Risk factors	0.1–0.4	Y	0.1–0.5	E	S	M	M	NA	NA	L	L	M	L–M	L	H

N = No Y = Yes D = Difficult E = Easy H = Heavy M = Moderate S = Slight	H = High M = Medium L = Low NA = Not applicable	H = High M = Medium L = Low

Table 5. Technique Applications

Techniques	Risk Identification	Risk Quantification	Risk Response Development
Analogy comparisons	●	○	○
Cost performance reports analysis	○	●	○
Cost risk/WBS simulation model	○	●	○
Decision analysis		●	○
Estimating relationships	○	●	
Expert interviews	●	○	○
Independent cost estimates	○	●	○
Independent technical assessment	●	○	○
Life-cycle cost analysis	○	●	○
Network analysis	○	●	○
Performance tracking	○		
Plan evaluation	●		
Project templates	●		○
Risk factors		●	○

● Predominant use
○ Secondary use

The chapters in Part II rate and discuss each risk analysis and assessment technique in the context of the previous criteria. The presentation will not make selecting a technique automatic, but it will provide project managers with an informed perspective to evaluate and choose an approach suited to the objectives of the risk management effort within the ever-present resource constraints of a project.

Extensive attention is paid to the selection criteria for each technique. Within the selection criteria, the three primary areas of analysis are resource requirements, applications, and output. The resource requirements include five subset areas of information for analysis:

- *Cost* refers to the cost of implementation in terms of resource-months.

- *Proper facilities and equipment* is an equally crucial issue. In most cases, the answer will be an attribute. Either a project has these facilities (Y) or it does not (N).

- *Time needed to implement* is, in part, a function of the information developed under the cost criterion. If fewer resources are available, the project may drag on much longer than anticipated. If more resources are available, the time required may be trimmed.

- *Ease of use* refers to the level of training and education required before the technique can be implemented. It may also refer to the level of effort that may be involved in simply implementing the technique. Ease of use is designated as easy (E), moderate (M), or difficult (D).

- *Project manager's time commitment* relates to the amount of oversight and involvement required by the project manager. If a project manager must make a long-term commitment, this level may be considered heavy (H). If it does not require an extensive commitment, the project manager's involvement may be slight (S) or moderate (M).

In the requirements for applications, each area is evaluated on the level of support the technique can provide: high (H), medium (M), or low (L). There are seven subsets of information:

- *Project status reporting* refers to monitoring plans, costs, and schedules to ensure that standards are met and problems are identified for timely corrective action.

- *Major planning decisions* are those decisions in which a project manager may be willing to invest significant resources and personal attention.

- *Contract strategy selection* typically occurs several times throughout the life of a project. Different techniques can bring extensive influence to bear on the types of contracts selected for any given project.

- *Milestone preparation* is the development of significant and appropriate milestones within any project. Some techniques can facilitate this process, others cannot.

- *Design guidance* refers to the level of insight the technique under consideration can potentially provide for any given project.

- *Source selection* is the effort to determine which sources may be potential vendors for the project. The level of guidance a technique can provide in this area may range from nonexistent to significant.

- *Budget submittal* is the final area of concern under application. Many tools are financially oriented and have the ability to generate copious financial data. Other techniques are not financially oriented. A technique's ability to contribute to an accurate assessment of the project budget is evaluated here.

The last area reviewed in each technique's selection is the output, in terms of information. As with the applications issues, ratings here are high (H), medium (M), or low (L). In this area, three primary issues are considered:

- *Accuracy* deals with the basic theoretical soundness of a technique and the presence of weakening assumptions that may dilute the value of information obtained in the analysis. Most techniques present an obvious trade-off between ease of use or time commitment and the accuracy of analysis results.

- *Level of detail* concerns the extent to which the output provides insight into cost, schedule, and technical risks. Techniques and how they are applied vary in the breadth, depth, and understanding that the output yields.

- *Utility* is a subjective factor that rates the output in a general context of its usefulness to the project manager. Both the effort involved and the value of information are considered.

It is important to note that some techniques have more applicability to specific project phases than do others. Likewise, the techniques do not all yield the same information. Each technique's applicability for each project phase and the type of information likely to result is indicated in Table 6. This table is a general summary; specific applications will continue to be exceptions to the guidance represented in it. Both project phase and the type of information desired must be considered in technique selection. For example, although networks do

Table 6. Project Phase Technique Application

Techniques	Project Phase				Information Yield				
	Concept	Development	Implementation	Closeout	Technology	Program	Support	Cost	Schedule
Analogy comparisons	o	+	+	+	+	o	o	+	o
Cost risk/WBS simulation model	–	–	+	+	–	–	–	+	–
Decision analysis	+	+	o	o	o	o	o	o	o
Estimating relationships	–	–	–	o	–	–	–	+	–
Expert interviews	+	+	+	+	+	o	+	o	o
Life-cycle cost analysis	–	o	o	+	–	–	+	+	–
Network analysis	–	+	+	o	+	o	+	+	+
Performance tracking	o	+	+	+	+	o	+	+	+
Plan evaluation	–	o	+	+	+	o	+	–	–
Project templates	o	+	+	+	+	o	+	–	–
Risk factors	–	o	+	+	–	–	–	+	–

– = Relatively weak
o = Average
+ = Relatively strong

not help analyze risks for repetitive processes, they have great value in planning and control to set up such processes.

Each chapter of Part II opens with a thorough discussion of a specific technique. The evaluation on the remaining pages of each chapter summarizes key characteristics to consider in selecting the appropriate technique.

Chapter 4

EXPERT INTERVIEWS

Obtaining accurate judgments from technical experts is one of the most critical elements in risk identification and risk quantification because of the following:

- The information identifies areas that are perceived as risky.

- The interviews provide the basis for taking qualitative information and transforming it into quantitative risk estimates.

Reliance on technical expertise is mandatory, because all information necessary for an accurate risk assessment usually cannot be derived from previous project data. However, obtaining the information from experts can be frustrating and often leads to less than optimum results.

Nearly all risk analysis techniques require some expert judgment. But it can be difficult to distinguish between good and bad judgment. This aspect makes the approach and documentation even more important than usual. The project manager or risk analyst performing the task is likely to get several divergent opinions from many "experts," and the project manager must be able to defend the ultimate position taken.

Technique Description

The expert interview technique is relatively simple. Basically, it consists of identifying appropriate experts and then methodically questioning them about risks in their areas of expertise as related to the project. (Many methods of doing this are outlined in Appendix D.) The technique can be used with individuals or groups of experts. The process normally obtains information on risk associated with all three sides of the triple constraint: schedule, cost, and performance.

When Applicable

This technique is recommended for all projects. Expert interviews focus on extracting information about what risks exist and how severe they may be. Interviews are most useful in risk identification but may apply in other processes as well. When questioning experts about risks on a project, it is logical to pursue potential risk responses and alternatives as well as information pertaining to probability and potential impact.

Input and Output

Expert interviewing has two prerequisites. First, the interviewer must prepare by researching the topic and thinking through the interview agenda. Second, the interviewee must be willing to spend the time necessary to divulge the information to the analyst or manager. Results of such interviews can be qualitative, quantitative, or both. Expert interviews nearly always result in input that can be used to develop a watchlist. They may also result in formulation of a range of uncertainty or a probability density function (PDF) for use in any of several risk analysis tools. The range or function can be expressed in terms of cost, schedule, or performance.

Major Steps in Applying the Technique

Because expert interviews result in a collection of subjective judgments, the only real error would be in the methodology used for gathering the data. If the techniques used are inadequate, then the entire risk identification and quantification process will be less reliable. Unfortunately, no technique exists for ensuring that the best possible data are collected. Several methodologies are available, but many must be eliminated because of time constraints. One combination that seems to work well consists of the following five steps:

- *Identify the right individual(s)*: Identifying the correct subject matter expert is extremely important. It is relatively easy to make a mistake and choose an expert who knows only a portion of the subject matter. If any doubt exists about the level of expertise, it is worthwhile to find one or two other candidates. The time used to identify individuals to interview will be well spent. Preliminary screening by telephone usually lasts only a few minutes and can give the analyst a sense of the interviewee's level of expertise and can help provide focus as questions are developed for the interview.

- *Prepare for the interview:* Participants save time if they all prepare adequately. Both interviewer and interviewee must consider what areas to cover during the interview. The interviewer must know and practice the methodology that will be used to quantify the expert judgment and should develop an agenda or topics list to ensure that the discussion has clear direction. In addition, the interviewer should understand how the expert functions in the organization and how long he or she has been in the field. The interviewer must keep the ultimate goals of risk identification and quantification in mind while preparing. This requires some time during the interview to allow the expert to offer personal thoughts on areas that may be outside his or her field.

- *Target the interest area:* The first portion of the actual interview will focus on verifying the previously identified risk areas. This should be kept brief, unless there appears to be disagreement that would require additional information. Next, the interview should move to the individual's area of expertise. This will confirm that the correct individual is being interviewed, and more time can then be spent gathering information. If the interviewer discovers that a "wrong" expert is being interviewed, the interview can be changed or ended, saving valuable time.

- *Solicit judgments and general information:* It is important to allow time for the expert to discuss other areas of the project after completing the target interest areas. If nothing else, the information gained can be used when interviewing other experts to stimulate thoughts and generate alternative opinions. Someone familiar with one area may identify risks in another area, because in some cases, those working in an area fraught with risks may be oblivious to those risks. This information generally becomes more refined as more subject matter experts are interviewed. Experience shows that if the expert is cooperative, the information given is generally accurate. Although additional clarification may be required or the expert may be unwilling to attempt quantification, identification of risk remains valid.

- *Quantify the information:* This may be the most sensitive aspect of any risk analysis. After risk areas have been identified, an estimate of their potential impact on the project cost, schedule, and performance must be made. This requires that the expert consider the probability of a given risk event's occurring and its potential impact.

Use of Results

Normally, the results of expert interviews feed other techniques or are used in developing watchlists, as described in "Products of Risk Quantification" in Chapter 3.

Resource Requirements

Conducting an expert interview is a relatively easy task. Virtually anyone can ask a series of questions and note responses. To generate *high-quality* data, however, the participants in the interview must *both* have some fundamental qualities. The interviewer must have the ability to assimilate information without bias and to report that information accurately and effectively in the context of the greater risk analysis. The interviewee must have the subject matter expertise directly related to the risk issues under consideration. If either of the parties lacks these fundamental skills, the expert interview will not be wholly effective.

Reliability

When conducted properly, expert interviews provide very reliable qualitative information. Transforming qualitative information into quantitative distributions or other measures depends on the skill of the interviewer. The technique is not without problems. Some of the types of problems experienced risk analysts have dealt with are as follows:

- Wrong expert identified
- Poor-quality information obtained
- Unwillingness of the expert to share information
- Changing opinions
- Conflicting judgments

Selection Criteria

As with each of the chapters on techniques, the expert interview technique is assessed against selection criteria relating to resource requirements, applications, and output for the technique. To compare expert interviews with other techniques, review Table 4.

Resource Requirements

What resources a technique requires is often the dominant consideration in the selection process. Interviewing experts requires two specific resources. The first is time. Although interviewing is one of the most common techniques for risk identification and quantification, it frequently is misapplied because of time limitations. Planned interviews are sometimes shortened or skipped altogether. Methodically examining an entire project requires the time of many experts—from both the project organization and the customer organization.

The second resource requirement is an interviewer. Frequently, experts give information that is not readily usable for a watchlist or probability density function. Some modest skill is required to encourage the expert to divulge information in the right format. If an interviewer lacks this skill, the techniques can still yield *some* valuable information if enough time is taken.

- *Cost* for expert interviews may range from minimal (1 to 2 days) to expansive (2 to 3 months), depending on the needs of the project. The more skilled the interviewer, the less time required to accomplish the same level of depth in expert interviewing. Thus, it often behooves the project manager to pay a little more for a qualified interviewer for a shorter period of time.

- *Proper facilities and equipment* for expert interviews are generally minimal, unless the interviews must be formally maintained. For a normal expert interview, the equipment will be no more involved than a few chairs, a pad of paper, and a tape recorder. In the extreme, an expert interview may feature a bank of television cameras and a recording studio. For the most part, expert interviews tend to be relatively easy to manage in terms of equipment and facilities.

- The *time needed to implement* an expert interview is a crucial consideration. But if resources and facilities are available, the time should not be extensive. In this case, because there are normally only one or two expert interviewers, the time to implement is reflected in the time required under "Cost."

- *Ease of use* is one of the most attractive features of expert interviews, because virtually anyone can conduct a passable interview with minimal training. The key, however, comes in developing interviewers who are truly skilled enough to draw out deeper and more meaningful responses from the interviewees. The most effective interviewers are those who can stage a relatively open-ended question and get back a clear and specific response. One way to achieve that is by listening carefully to the answers and providing feedback to clarify any outstanding issues.

■ The *project manager's time commitment* is sometimes based on the skill levels of the project manager as an expert interviewer. Assessed on a gradient of slight to moderate to heavy, as long as the project manager is not personally required to conduct the interviews or train the interviewers, the time required of the project manager is slight.

Applications

As stated earlier, the expert interview has the advantage of being applicable in a wide variety of situations. The applicability of the interviews is assessed on a scale of high, medium, and low.

■ *Project status reporting* refers to monitoring plans, costs, and schedules. Although the monitoring process is not a primary application of the expert interview, gathering the information essential to status reports is often a function of the interviews. From that perspective, project status reports would be difficult (if not impossible) to develop without some interviewing skills.

■ *Major planning decisions* often hinge on the opinions of a few key individuals associated with the project. As such, the expert interview may expedite the process and ensure full participation with the individuals involved.

■ *Contract strategy selection* does not rely as heavily on expert interviews as it does on other techniques, but the interviews can play a valuable role in building the support data to feed those other techniques.

■ Applying expert interviews in *milestone preparation* is direct and important. Because the objectives are to ensure that planning has been comprehensive and the system is ready to move forward into its next phase, in-depth consultation with both internal and external customers is vital.

■ *Design guidance* is useful for decisions ranging from considering technology alternatives for major systems to choosing components. To understand how uncertainties relate to one another and how the alternatives compare, expert interviews are often used in the data-gathering stage.

- *Source selection* is a prime application for expert interviews. In many cases, interviews determine which candidates to eliminate for a subcontract or consulting position. In addition, if the expert interview is conducted properly during source selection, it can open new avenues for later negotiation with the source.

- *Budget submittal* is a crucial step in project management, but it is not well supported by expert interviews, because budgets work almost exclusively from purely quantifiable data.

Output

The output of the expert interview is most often a collection of notes or an individual's evaluation and documentation of those notes, organized in a comprehensible fashion. The output can include both qualitative data and individual perspectives on quantitative data.

- *Accuracy* deals with the basic theoretical soundness of expert interviewing. Because it is considered by many to be extremely easy with a limited time commitment, the accuracy is often called into question. The accuracy is only as good as the interviewer *and* the interviewee. If they are both well versed in their respective skill areas, the interview can have high accuracy. If they have limited skill levels, the interview may have low accuracy. Generally, the expert interview must be considered less than purely quantitative.

- *Level of detail* is not the greatest strength of an expert interview, but interviews may provide incredible depth that is not achievable through other techniques. Interviews may also be so superfluous that the information is useless. Once again, the talents of the resources drive the ultimate level of detail.

- *Utility* is a subjective factor that takes into account both the effort involved and the value of the information. For most expert interviews, the documentation developed after completing the interviews becomes a crucial element in the project's records.

Summary

In determining the effectiveness of expert interviews, it is vital to evaluate the skills of both the interviewer and the interviewee. That information provides the best sense of how well (and how accurately) the insights required will be developed. Although the expert interview can be reasonably handled (even by team members with limited skill sets), the best results will be presented by those who understand the critical nature of the expert interview and the myriad applications for the technique.

Chapter 5

ANALOGY COMPARISON

The analogy comparison and lessons-learned techniques for risk identification and quantification are based on the idea that no project, no matter how advanced or unique, represents a totally new system. Most projects originated or evolved from existing projects or simply represent a new combination of existing components or subsystems. A logical extension of this premise is that the project manager can gain key insights concerning various aspects of a current project's risk by examining the successes, failures, problems, and solutions of similar existing or past projects. The experience and knowledge gained, or lessons learned, can be applied to the task of identifying potential risk in a project and developing a strategy to handle that risk.

Technique Description

The analogy comparison and lessons-learned techniques involve identifying past or existing programs similar to the current project effort and reviewing and using data from these projects in the risk process. The term *similar* refers to the commonality of various characteristics that define a project. The analogy may be similar in technology, function, contract strategy, manufacturing process, or other area. The key is to understand the relationships among the project characteristics and the particular aspects of the project being examined. For example, in many system developments, historical cost data show a strong positive relationship with technical complexity. Thus, when looking for a project in which to analyze cost risk for comparison, it makes sense to examine data from projects with similar function, technology, and technical complexity. The use of data or lessons learned from past programs may be applicable at the system, subsystem, or component level. For example, although an existing system's function and quantity produced differ, its processor may be similar in performance characteristics to that of a current project, thereby making the processor a valid basis for analogy comparison. Several different projects may be used for comparison to the current project at various levels of the end item.

When Applicable

Project managers can apply lessons learned or compare existing projects to new projects in all phases and aspects of a project any time historical data are useful. These techniques are especially valuable when a system is primarily a new combination of existing subsystems, equipment, or components. The value increases significantly when recent and complete historical project data are available. When properly done and documented, analogy comparison provides a good understanding of how project characteristics affect risks identified and serves as necessary input to other risk techniques.

Input and Output

Three types of data are required to use the technique:

- Description and project characteristics of the new system and its components (or approach)

- Description and project characteristics of the existing or past projects and their components (or approach)

- Detailed data (cost, schedule, and performance) for the previous system being reviewed

The description and project characteristics are needed to draw valid analogies between the current and past projects. The detailed data are required to evaluate and understand project risks and their potential effect on the current project.

Often the project manager needs technical specialists to make appropriate comparisons and to help extrapolate or adjust the data from old projects to make inferences about new projects. Technical or project judgments may be needed to adjust findings and data for differences in complexity, performance, physical characteristics, or contracting approach.

The output from examining analogous projects and lessons learned typically becomes the input to other risk assessment and analysis techniques. The review of project lessons-learned reports can identify a number of problems to be integrated into a project's watchlist. The length and volatility of past development projects provide information that helps build realistic durations in a network analysis of a new project's development schedule. Data from the lessons-learned review become the source of information for risk identification, quantification, and response techniques.

Major Steps in Applying the Technique

The major steps in using analogous system data and lessons learned include identifying analogous programs, collecting data, and analyzing the data gathered. Figure 11 shows a further breakdown of this process.

The first step is to determine the information needs in this phase of risk management. Information needs can range from preliminary risk assessment on a key approach to a project-wide analysis of major risks associated with the effort. The second step is to define the basic characteristics of the new system. With the new system generally defined, the analyst can begin to identify past projects with similar attributes for comparison and analysis.

The next steps in this process, being interdependent, are generally done in parallel. The key to useful analogy comparisons is the availability of data on past projects. The new system is broken down into logical components for comparison while assessing the availability of historical data. The same level of detailed information is necessary to make comparisons. Based on the availability of data, the information needs of the process, and the logical structure of the project, analogous systems are selected and data are gathered.

The data gathered for comparison include the detailed information being analyzed as well as the general characteristics and descriptions of the past projects. The general project description data are essential to ensure that proper analogies are being drawn and that the relationship between these characteristics and the detailed data being gathered is clear. For the analogy to be valid, some relationship must exist between the characteristic being used to make comparisons and the specific aspect of the project being examined.

Often the data collection process and initial assessment lead to further defining the system for the purposes of comparison. After this is accomplished, the last step in the process is analyzing and normalizing

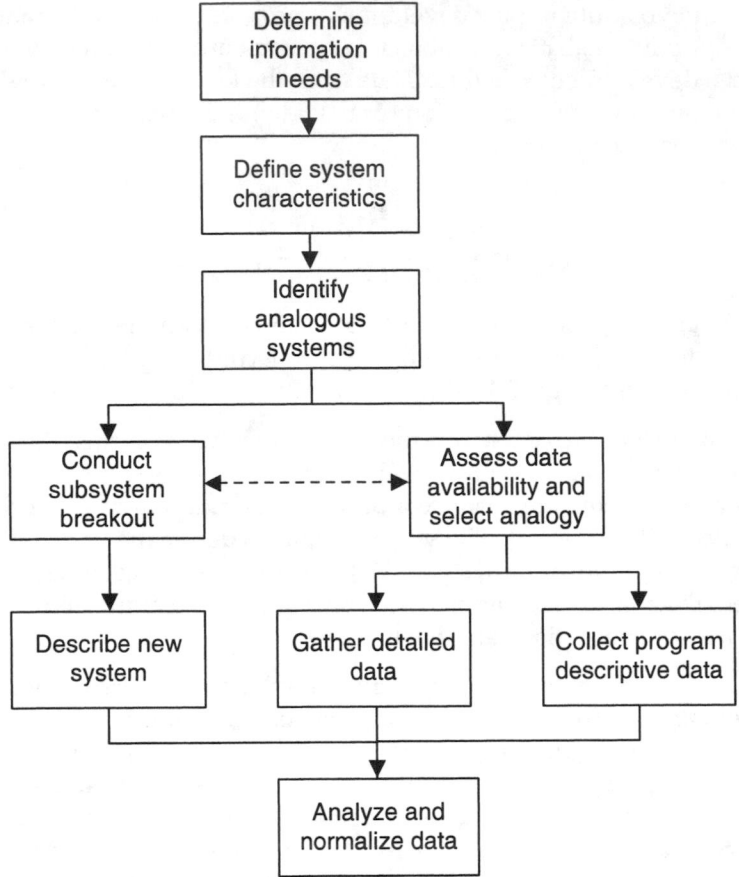

Figure 11. Analogy Comparison

the historical data. Comparisons to older systems may not be exact. The data may need to be adjusted to serve as a basis for estimating the current project. For example, in analogy-based cost estimating, cost data must be adjusted for inflation, overhead rates, general and administrative (G&A) rates, and so on, for accurate comparison. Project managers frequently require technical assistance to adjust data for differences between past and current projects. The desired output is some insight into the cost, schedule, and technical risks of a project based on observations of similar past projects.

Use of Results

As stated earlier, the output from analogies and lessons learned typically augments other risk techniques. The results may provide a checklist of factors to monitor for the development of problems or a range of cost factors to use in estimating. Analogies and lessons learned generate risk information. Whether the information is used in a detailed estimate, in a technology trade-off study, or at a system level for a quick test of reasonableness, the results are intended to provide the analyst with insights for analysis and decision making.

Resource Requirements

Using analogous data and lessons-learned studies to gather risk data is a relatively easy task. Selecting proper comparisons and analyzing the data gathered may require some technical assistance and judgment but probably not beyond the capabilities of the project manager. The time and effort needed for an analogy comparison can vary widely. The resources required depend on the depth of the data gathering, the number of different projects, and the availability of historical data. A project team can expend much effort for a limited amount of information. That is why an initial assessment of data availability is important in selecting analogous programs to compare.

Reliability

The use of analogy comparisons and lessons learned has two limitations. The first, availability of data, has already been discussed. If common project characteristics cannot be found or if detailed data are missing from either the old or new systems, the data collected will have limited utility. The second limitation deals with the accuracy of the analogy drawn. An older system may be somewhat similar, but rapid changes in technology, manufacturing, methodology, and so on, may make comparisons inappropriate.

Selection Criteria

As with each of the chapters on techniques, analogy comparison is assessed against selection criteria relating to resource requirements, applications, and output for this technique. To compare analogies with other techniques, review Table 4.

Resource Requirements

- The *cost* associated with the analogy comparison techniques is relatively low if the organization has been fastidious about retaining information from past projects. If there is a broad database from which to draw information, the analogy techniques can easily be applied, assuming that the new project is, even in part, analogous to an older project. Unfortunately, most new projects are not wholly analogous and must be evaluated against piecemeal information. If the data are available, the resource time consumed may be as little as a week or less. If the data are sketchy, it can take multiple resource-months to gather the data from the various departments or projects within the organization.

- *Proper facilities and equipment* are rudimentary, consisting of little more than a personal computer loaded with the appropriate word processing and project management applications.

- The *time needed to implement* this approach is a direct function of the number of sources from which data are available and the number of team resources assigned to the activity. With a team of three or four data gatherers, even the most complex set of information may be compiled and reviewed in as little as a week or two. With a single individual assigned to the task, the resource-hours assigned in the "Cost" category apply.

- *Ease of use* appears to be a major advantage to the analogy approach, but that ease can be deceptive. Some project managers will be tempted to make across-the-board, one-for-one analogies for the entire project. That is applicable only in the rarest of cases. The technique is only appropriate if it is applied in the context of the new project under consideration. This may be evaluated in terms of the scale of the projects being compared, the time frames in which they are developed or the resources applied against both. This technique often appears easier than it is.

- The *project manager's time commitment* in this technique is a factor of how heavily involved the project manager wishes to become in analyzing the data. If the project manager wants to spend as little time as possible approving the work of the team, the level of effort is nominal. It is recommended, however, that the project manager invest at least several hours analyzing the analogous projects driving the conclusions.

Applications

- For *project status reporting,* the analogy comparison technique has little value. It can serve only as defense of certain numbers that may have been used to establish the baseline for the project. Otherwise, analogy comparisons have little value when assessing the new project's current status.

- *Major planning decisions* should rely very heavily on an organization's lessons learned. History is an excellent teacher, and using the organization's historic experience with similar projects can prove invaluable. If certain approaches have been attempted, it is vital to find out whether they succeeded or failed.

- As with planning decisions, the issue of *contract strategy selection* can also be developed using analogy comparison techniques. If work with a similar client, similar project, or similar resources has failed, in part, by using one contract strategy, it is worthwhile to consider alternate strategies.

- *Milestone preparation* is not an area in which analogy comparisons have much value, unless a project was noted as exceptional in part because of the outstanding use of milestones. Milestones are rarely major influences in a project's success or failure. In the rare case in which milestones *have* played a key role, the analogy technique may apply.

- Although *design guidance* does not rely exclusively on analogy comparisons, it should be a key component of any design decision. Too often, organizations fail to scrutinize the failings of past designs, only to learn the project at hand is failing for the same reasons as a project just a year or two before. Analogy comparisons will not provide the complete picture on design guidance, but it will provide a sense of corporate history and experience.

- Many organizations, including the U.S. government, are making analogy comparisons a key component of *source selection.* Terms like past performance, performance history, and preferred vendor all reflect some analysis of analogous projects. These are valuable analyses, because organizations should not make the mistake of dealing with a less-than-acceptable vendor more than once.

- For *budget submittal,* the analogy comparisons technique has limited application except as a background for some of the numbers that may have been incorporated into the budget. Although analogies may be found, some independent extrapolation or evaluation of the data must also be conducted.

Output

- *Accuracy* of the analogy comparison technique is less than ideal. The technique relies not only on the accuracy of past data but also on the accuracy of the interpretation of that data, which incorporates two variables into the overall assessment of the data for the new project. Thus, the level of accuracy comes into question.

- The *level of detail* generated by the technique is almost a direct function of the volume of data stored by the organization. If an organization is meticulous in its project recordkeeping, the level of detail can be tremendous. If, however, the organization has a limited, purely anecdotal history, the level of detail becomes low, at best.

- The *utility* of the output is based on both the quality of the analogous documentation and the relevance of the analogy. If both are high quality, the information obtained has the potential to be extremely useful. If, however, the relevance or quality are in question, the usefulness diminishes significantly.

Summary

In evaluating the potential use of analogy comparisons for an organization, the first step should always be an assessment of the volume and quality of the documentation to be used for analogies, including how recent it is. If the organization does not effectively maintain this information, the analogy comparison technique may prove useless for virtually any application.

Chapter 6

PLAN EVALUATION

This technique highlights and isolates risks caused by disparities in planning. It evaluates project plans for contradictions and voids. Traditional, formal plans used to guide a project include the following:

- Project
- Quality
- Communication

- Contracting
- Testing
- Training

Other documents are also key to the success of the project:

- Work breakdown structure
- Project specifications

- Statement of work (SOW)
- Contracts
- Other baseline documents

Although plans outline project implementation steps, other documents represent critical communication with stakeholders about what is to be done. Flaws, inconsistencies, contradictions, and voids in these documents inevitably lead to project problems and introduce significant risk. Figure 12 illustrates the linkage between three key documents.

Technique Description

The plan evaluation technique simply suggests a thorough, recurring review of all plans—internally—for correctness, completeness, and currency, with a cross-check for consistency.

Using the WBS for Risk Identification

Proper development of a WBS represents a major step in risk control. It constitutes much of the project definition. Its quality, indeed its very existence, provides the planning framework that sets the standard for

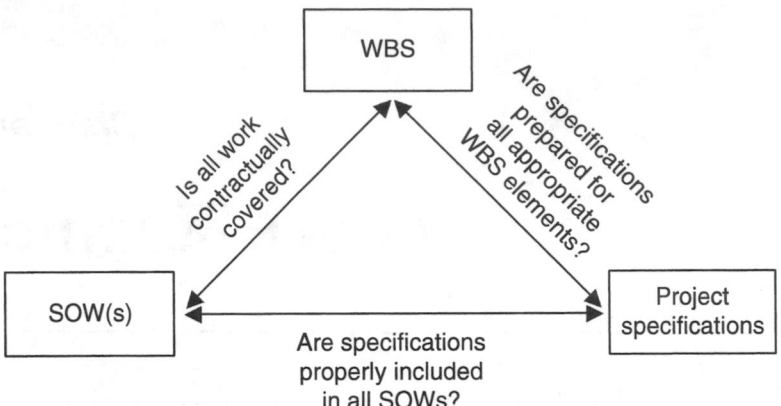

Figure 12. Plan Evaluation Technique

the future of the project. As a WBS is completed, a careful examination is appropriate:

- Are all elements of the WBS necessary and sufficient?

- Is there a WBS dictionary, and does it adequately explain the content of each element?

- Does the WBS represent what is to be done rather than who is to do it?

- Are all elements of the WBS present?

- Is the contracting strategy reflected in the project WBS?

- Is any work to be done that is not reflected in the WBS?

The WBS offers a framework for organizing and displaying risk factors. The technique of downward allocation and upward summarization through the WBS can be used to highlight discrepancies in most of the project's performance parameters, such as efficiency, reliability, cost, and capability.

The WBS provides a sensible structure for treating technical risk. A systematic review of each WBS element for risk identification and preliminary rating will yield much information to the risk analyst.

The relationship between the WBS and the specifications is so important that mapping the relationships is a valuable exercise for the risk analyst. Mapping will highlight inconsistencies between the work to be done and the performance to be achieved.

The project WBS eventually becomes the aggregate of all contract information, including subcontractors' plans. The risk analyst should review the WBS with the question "Who is doing what?" as a test of reasonableness of the contracting strategy. Finally, the WBS represents the framework for cost and schedule performance. A survey of both cost and schedule reporting in the context of the WBS identifies possible blind spots in cost and schedule information. As part of this survey, the analyst can gain valuable insights by comparing the numbering schemes for the WBS, scheduling system, and cost-reporting system. Ease of translation among and ease of summarization within each of these numbering systems indicate how well traceability among the WBS, schedules, and cost data can be maintained. Incompatibility introduces management risk into the project.

Using Specifications for Risk Identification

Some of the previous discussion deals with the important relationship between the WBS and the specifications and the need for compatibility. When that compatibility exists, the performance to be achieved can be related to the work to be done. Because the specifications represent the source of all technical performance requirements, they are the single most important source of information for the risk analyst attempting to identify, organize, and display items of technical risk. Each performance parameter of a given WBS element represents a possible focus for an expert interview on technical risk.

As with the WBS, a survey of the specifications is appropriate for risk identification:

- Do the specifications overlay the WBS so that performance requirements are specified for WBS elements?

- Are all performance parameters identified even though they may not be specified (that is, given a discrete value)?

- Can the risk of achieving the specified value for the performance parameter be sensibly discussed?

- Is there a technical performance measurement scheme for each performance parameter?

Using Statements of Work for Risk Identification

The SOW is the single most important communication between the project organization and the customer. If the WBS and the specifications are complete and well developed, SOWs are fairly straightforward. The risk analyst is searching primarily for gaps in coverage and should consider the following:

- Does the SOW cover whole parts of the WBS that can be clearly evaluated against the specifications?

- Does the SOW represent work that matches the project organization in terms of politics, contractual capabilities, and legal capabilities?

- Is all work contractually covered?

- Are the SOW requirements properly related to the specification?

Developing a Technical Risk Dictionary

A dictionary in project management can expand understanding and provide documentation and background on specific areas of projects. Thus far, this chapter has addressed the need to gather all project information into a common database, with common descriptions. A technical risk dictionary, as conceptualized in Figure 13, offers the risk analyst a single place to gather this information to facilitate the risk identification and definition processes.

Creating a technical risk dictionary has been a formidable editorial task until recently. Advances in project management software coupled with advances in word processing and documentation software allow for integrating data within a single database. In many cases, proper use of the project management software can facilitate generating a technical risk dictionary with a single macro.

The use of automated tools (Project Scheduler, Microsoft Project, CA-SuperProject, Project Workbench, ARTEMIS Prestige, Primavera Project Planner, and so on) has facilitated integrating risk management and project management practice. Because these tools afford data storage space for text to integrate risk identification with specific tasks, summary tasks, systems, and phases, project managers are better able to identify and manage risk in their daily operations.

Using Other Plans for Risk Identification

"Risk Identification," in Chapter 3, discusses the use of a top-level risk matrix to highlight and isolate risks. The matrix relies heavily on goal definition and strategy development. The presumption is that

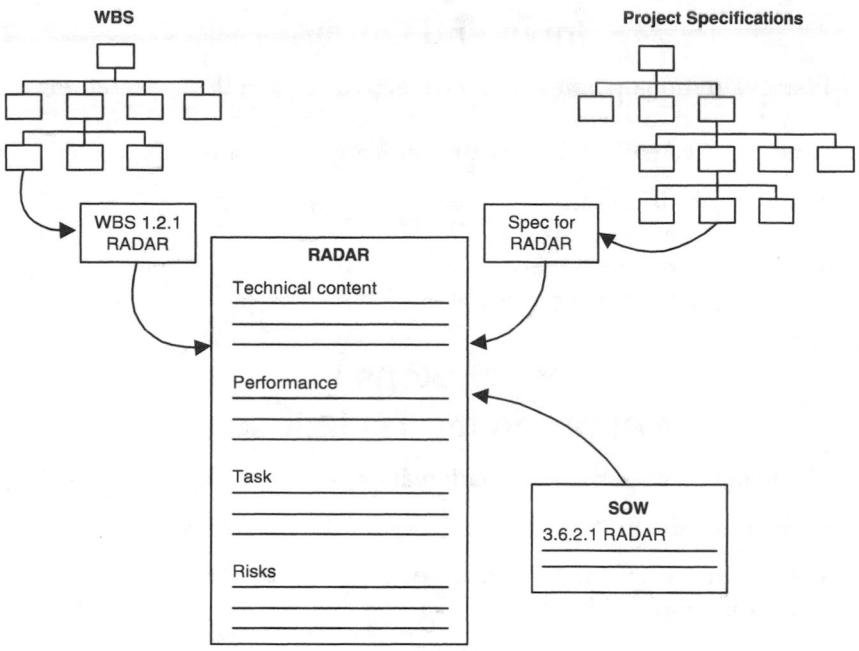

Figure 13. Technical Risk Dictionary

the strategies expressed in the project plans are directed at meeting the project goals. Comparing the two can identify risks. The same thinking can be applied to lower-level risk matrices associated with any other plans (communication, quality, testing, and so on) developed.

When Applicable

The plan evaluation technique is directed specifically at risk identification and is best used for technical risk. Its utility for cost and schedule risk is considerably lower. However, this technique could highlight missing information concerning deliverables that would affect cost and schedule risks. It is most applicable to the implementation phase of a project. As a risk identification technique, it requires the existence of the plans to be evaluated. As a risk avoidance tool, it can be used during the project planning process.

Input and Output

Plan evaluation operates on the collective body of documentation broadly referred to as project plans and includes primarily those documents listed earlier. The output typically is as follows:

- Top-level risk matrix
- Lower-level risk matrices
- Technical risk dictionary
- Updated version of project plans

Major Steps in Applying the Technique

The major steps in plan evaluation are as follows:

- Evaluate the WBS for completeness and correctness

- Evaluate specifications for completeness, correctness, and compatibility with the WBS

- Evaluate SOWs for completeness, correctness, and compatibility with the WBS and for inclusion of specification references

- Evaluate other plans, and develop a lower-level risk matrix for each

Use of Results

Plan evaluation is designed to improve the quality of and reduce the risks associated with the project plan. The technique also produces descriptive documentation on the technical performance, programmatic risks, and supportability risks associated with the project. The technical risk dictionary describes technical risks in a centralized location. This technique can produce a single "official" list (a watchlist) of project risks that will receive active management attention.

Resource Requirements

This technique requires a great deal of thought and experienced, knowledgeable personnel who are thoroughly familiar with the content of the total project. The project manager (or deputy) leading a team of senior staff members would constitute the ideal team for this technique.

Reliability

The reliability of plan evaluation is driven by the completeness and the farsightedness of the project plans. If the myriad support plans are all well defined for a low-risk project, only a handful of project risks will be uncovered. If the support plans are well defined for a higher-risk project, there is a likelihood of numerous risks.

The major caution for using this technique is to avoid forcing detailed project definition too early. Some inconsistencies exist because of poor planning, but others exist because of a legitimate lack of information.

Selection Criteria

As with each of the chapters on techniques, plan evaluation is assessed against selection criteria relating to resource requirements, applications, and output for the technique. To compare plan evaluation with other techniques, review Table 4.

Resource Requirements

- With plan evaluations, *cost* constraints are extremely flexible. If the project manager determines that a comprehensive review of every piece of project planning documentation is appropriate, numerous resources will be required for an extended period of time. If, by contrast, the project manager determines that a high-level summary review is appropriate, the resources required will drop significantly. In this chapter, the discussion has focused on in-depth analyses, so the assumption is that the analysis will be comprehensive. In this scenario, a comprehensive evaluation may prove to be prohibitively costly, because key resources will be required to justify their existing plans and reevaluate the plans' efficacy. To do a comprehensive evaluation, each team member responsible for a component plan will have to spend several days to a week analyzing their documentation and documenting those analyses. Using the full complement of plans described at the beginning of the chapter, an effort for a 1-year period may require 4 to 6 resource-weeks.

- *Proper facilities and equipment* are limited to enough personal computers to support all team members involved in the review.

Team members will need access to the master planning documentation, including the supporting documents (which would require a word processing application) and the project management software program and files. This technique is not equipment intensive.

■ The *time needed to implement* this approach is highly dependent on the number of resources applied. To be effective, one resource should be designated for each major piece of documentation to be evaluated. However, most organizations are not willing to commit that level of staff to a single evaluation effort. Thus, the work will be spread across a more limited base. In the ideal, this effort should be accomplished in 2 or 3 days, with a skilled, broad-based team. With fewer resources, the effort may take as long as 4 to 6 resource-weeks.

■ *Ease of use* is an issue with this technique, because the project manager will clearly understand the level of effort required to analyze the output, but management and team members may not appreciate the in-depth analysis essential to a clear understanding of the information. For some team members and stakeholders, the entire package may present information that does not meet their specific needs. For others, the material may be presented in a way they cannot understand. The proper sorting and filtering of the information is vital to the ease of use for this technique for all its recipients.

■ The *project manager's time commitment* is significant. Because the project manager normally understands the details of the plans, he or she becomes the focal point for all questions and clarifications that team members require. The project manager's ready availability facilitates the efforts of the technical personnel responsible for their respective support plans or project plan components.

Applications

■ Plan evaluations are essential to *project status reporting*, because without a thorough review of the project plans and their variances to date, it is impossible to evaluate project status in an accurate, historic context. In many ways, plan evaluations almost force the project team into developing status reports, because that is the best application for the technique.

- *Major planning decisions* should also hinge on a sense of project history, and (as with status reporting) they may hinge on the evaluations of specific project plans. The difference in the application with major planning decisions is that major planning decisions may focus on one particular aspect of the project (such as schedule, cost, or performance) and thus may not require the level of depth described in this chapter. The planning decision may hinge on a single type of support plan or a single component of the project plan. Either way, plan evaluation ultimately provides ideal support in major planning decisions, whether from a component of the plan or from the comprehensive plan evaluation.

- Although *contract strategy selection* relies on the evaluation of the initial project plan, it is not normally considered a key application for plan evaluation. Plan evaluations are normally conducted after the project is being implemented to assess the effectiveness of the plan versus reality.

- As with contract strategy selection, *milestone preparation* is most often a step conducted at the beginning of the project. However, there is a slightly closer link between milestone preparation and plan evaluation than occurs with the contract strategy selection. Specifically, many plan evaluations will lead to corrective action, which often includes adding supplemental milestones to ensure that the corrective action is effective. As such, there is a modest correlation between this application and the technique.

- *Design guidance* can be supported by plan evaluations only during the early phases of the project and, even then, only to a limited degree. To provide guidance, the plans must show some direct link between the original design selected and the project plan or its supporting plans. If no such link exists, the plan evaluation technique does not apply.

- In *source selection*, there is little applicability for plan evaluation, unless the selection occurs at midproject or in the context of multiple projects. The plan evaluation technique can afford insights into the needs of the project and the shortcomings of the existing vendor base, but for initial source or vendor selection, there is little applicability.

- *Budget submittal* is not affected by the plan evaluation technique unless (as with source selection) the budget is an interim budget being submitted at midproject. In any other scenario, the plan evaluation technique has extremely limited applicability.

Output

- *Accuracy* is a cornerstone of the plan evaluation technique. It is wholly designed to discover inaccuracies and to address them. Although much of the evaluation is subjective, the results tend to make plans better reflect the project as it is evolving.

- The *level of detail* in the plan evaluation technique is exhaustive. The information drawn from the various plans and the assessment of those plans is most effectively done when all the plans are assessed for their effectiveness to date. Although a simple WBS review might require moderate scrutiny, the level of effort and the depth of information developed in a plan evaluation is extensive.

- For areas in which the plan evaluation technique is logically applied, its *utility* is extremely high. Unfortunately, project managers may be tempted to use the plan evaluation as a panacea for analyzing all project risk. Although the plan evaluation applies well in some areas, it is inappropriate in others. The evaluation data are so in-depth and diverse that they have the potential to be misinterpreted or misused.

Summary

In an ideal world, where a project manager is supported by seasoned professionals of long tenure, plan evaluations would produce few results for a significant level of effort. All planning documents would be created in proper sequence, each with reference to all that preceded it. Eminently logical contracts would be let with masterful work statements and perfect specifications. In reality, as team members shift in and out of projects and schedules and objectives change, plans often represent the only key to organizational memory. With planning conducted early in a project, any link to organizational memory later in the effort becomes significant.

The plan evaluation technique is extremely useful because of its clear strengths in so many applications and the relative value in terms of resource consumption and output. As long as the project manager uses the tool appropriately, it is one of the most powerful techniques available.

Chapter 7

PROJECT TEMPLATES

This technique is based on the precept that, in many organizations, templates exist to facilitate planning and to minimize risk. Templates are nothing more than fully developed plans, forms, or outlines that provide structure for an organization's project managers. These templates often manifest themselves as elements of a much larger project management methodology. By properly applying these templates (or even recognizing their existence), it becomes possible to mitigate additional risk and apply best practices to existing risks.

Technique Description

The technique consists of examining a series of templates covering specific areas that may present technical risk to a project. Each template examines an area of risk and then describes methods for avoiding or controlling that risk. Much of the risk description and the solution is based on lessons learned from other projects. The areas that may be covered by such templates are illustrated in Figure 14.

When Applicable

Project templates should be used for most projects—either independently or in conjunction with another technique. Organizational templates contain *extremely* valuable information, because they are based on actual experience. Templates are generally built as a response to past incidents, as a means to preclude a risk that has already befallen an organization. The information can be pertinent for any size project at any phase of development. Because the technique views project management as a complete process, the solutions presented reflect the interdependency of each part of the cycle. In other words, a conscious

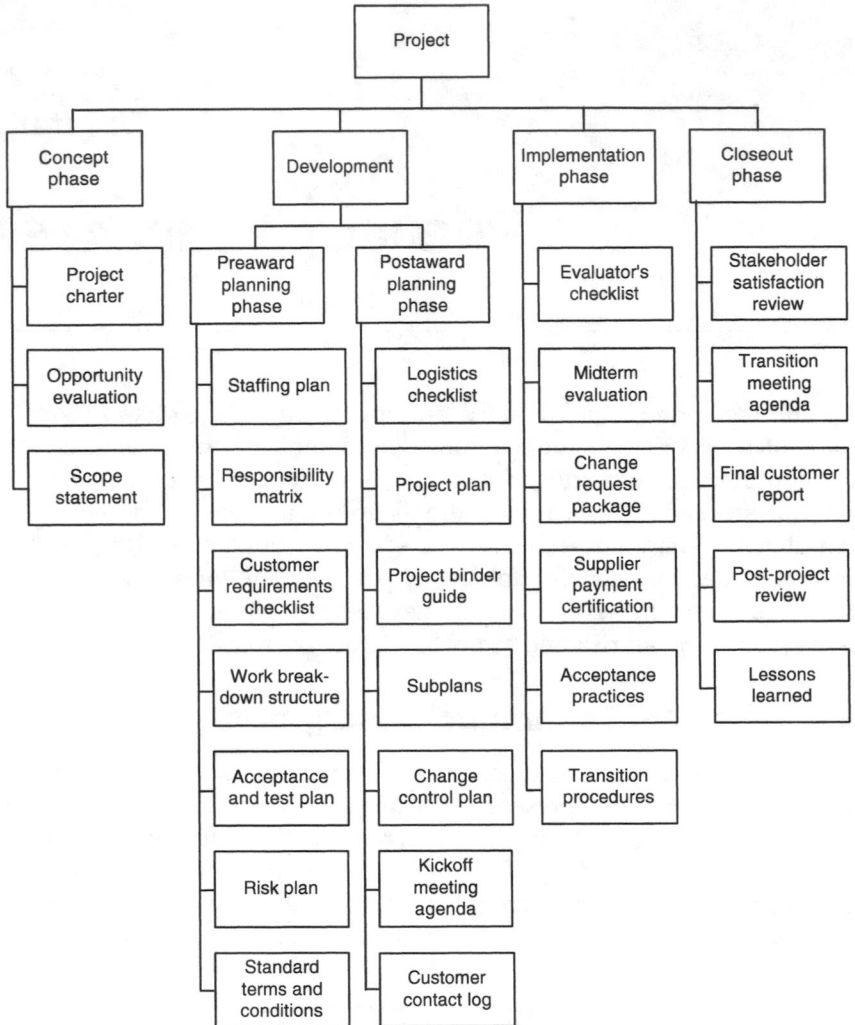

**Figure 14. Common Project Management
Templates, Arranged by Phase**

effort is made to present a solution that lowers the total risk for the
entire project, not just for short-term problems.

Input and Output

Because the technique is not a model, it requires no formal input.
What it does require is discipline. Time must be committed to reading

the templates and the organizational methodologies driving them and then to using that information to examine risk within a given project. A practical output of the technique is the watchlist described in "Products of Risk Quantification" in Chapter 3.

Major Steps in Applying the Technique

Because methodologies and templates cover areas common to nearly every project, each template should at least be reviewed. The project manager determines whether the template is appropriate to the project and its specific technical risks. After reviewing the template, the project manager or team member responsible should evaluate the project in terms of solutions or risk mitigating actions that the template would prescribe. A periodic review of all templates is recommended with updates as the project progresses.

Use of Results

Results from templates can be used in a variety of ways:

- In presentations to higher levels of authority
- To influence the team members' current level of activity in an area
- For continued monitoring of progress in each project area

Resource Requirements

Generally, templates require that the project manager be involved in the risk identification process. Input should be provided by all functional managers. The use of the templates is not intended to require substantial special skills or extra resources.

Reliability

Two cautions apply when using this technique:

- Project participants should not assume that templates contain all possible technical risks within a given area. Although common problems are identified, this is not an exhaustive list.

- Templates may not contain information regarding several programmatic risk areas that should also be examined.

Selection Criteria

As with each of the chapters on techniques, the project template technique is assessed against selection criteria relating to resource requirements, applications, and output for the technique. To compare project templates with other techniques, review Table 4.

Resource Requirements

- The additional *cost* associated with project templates is small. This technique requires little additional resourcing beyond what is normally necessary to manage a project properly. The time consumed is nominal as long as the work is done continuously and incrementally.

- There are no special equipment needs for this technique, because it is primarily a small administrative burden. For *proper facilities and equipment*, the only requirement is to find the files, databases, or shelves housing the information.

- The *time needed to implement* project templates is actually a function of the level of discipline of the project manager. Project templates must be reviewed (and comparative project progress analyzed) regularly against each of the template areas.

- Project templates have extremely good *ease of use*. They do not require special skills beyond being able to comprehend the information requested for each particular template. They are designed to prevent organizations from regenerating established protocols each time a new project arises.

- The *project manager's time commitment* to the templates is moderate, because the project manager invariably will spend some time selecting the appropriate templates for his or her project and will also be responsible for reviewing the templates as they are completed. The investment with respect to the return, however, is significant, because the project team develops information that virtually anyone in the organization's project support structure can understand.

Applications

Project templates can be used in most application categories in Table 4. The technique is only indirectly useful in the budget category, because it deals with preventive technical aspects rather than cost issues. It can, however, provide insight into the impetus behind both cost and subcontractor actions in situations involving vendors.

- For *project status reporting,* project managers often find it helpful to build their status reports in the formats designed by others. This convention of building from past efforts within the organization becomes more time- and cost-effective as the organization develops. As a project template, project status reports will inherently highlight some of the issues that have arisen in the past.

- *Major planning decisions* require a sense of organizational history. Project templates offer that information as well. If an organization has project templates in place either on an ad hoc basis or as part of a methodology, the templates can expose issues that have driven major decisions in the past.

- *Contract strategy selection* almost consistently has some type of existing templates. Project templates encourage consistency in contract development and organization from project to project.

- *Milestone preparation* often requires the use of project templates. Templates are often structured around milestones, specifically to meet client needs or reporting needs. Templates for these events are commonplace and thus become critical tools for the project manager. By using templates (such as closeout checklists, annual budget review formats, or decision-point analysis grids), the project manager can ensure that all the reports, components, or completion criteria for a particular milestone are prepared in a timely fashion.

- In terms of *design guidance,* project templates have clear utility, but there is a caveat. Project templates rely on history. Design is often driven by the latest developments in technology. As such, the information required by the template may not fit within current desired designs. In most cases, however, project templates are a good fit for design guidance, for even as technology changes, many of the same questions or issues continue to apply.

- *Source selection* requires rigorous procedures if vendors are to be assessed fairly and consistently. Project templates are those procedures.

- *Budget submittal* is not a clear use for project templates. Although the templates facilitate formatting, they do not generally include relevant historic cost data. That information can only be obtained through rigorous analysis.

Output

If the user properly documents results from a review of project templates, the output will provide a set of traceable management data that can be used to make sound decisions on a variety of customer, personnel, and technical issues.

- *Accuracy* of the project templates technique is a direct function of the adherence of the project manager to the approach. There is often a temptation to skip templates that don't seem to address the project at hand, but as that is done, it may result in missing key problem areas.

- The *level of detail* obtained through project templates can potentially be exhaustive. If there is a complete methodology, the project templates give the project manager a sense of all the risks faced by most of the project managers in the organization's past. It also provides a detailed examination of virtually all aspects of the organization. If a single template is used or only one area is covered, the level of detail can diminish significantly.

- The *utility* of project templates is in their capacity to save the project manager from rediscovering organizational issues that may have a negative effect on the project. Because such templates are normally based on the experience of an organization's more talented project managers, they save the current project manager from constantly evaluating and reevaluating the project and the organization to ensure that every potential risk area has been addressed.

Summary

With project templates, the key is discipline—the discipline required to go through the process in small, manageable steps. If a project manager or team attempts to complete all project templates at one time, the task will invariably be overwhelming and enormously time consuming. If, instead, the effort is conducted incrementally over time, the administrative burden is reduced and the technique becomes far less onerous for long-term utility and application.

Chapter 8

DECISION ANALYSIS

Decision analysis can be used to determine strategies when a decision maker is faced with several decision alternatives and an uncertain or risk-filled pattern of future events. Before selecting a specific decision analysis technique, the type of situation must be considered. Classifying decision-making situations is based on how much is known about those future events that are beyond the decision maker's control (known as states of nature). Thus, the two types of situations are as follows:

- Decision making under certainty (when states of nature are known)

- Decision making under uncertainty (when states of nature are unknown)

The decision analysis techniques appropriate for risk identification, quantification, and prioritization are those that consider decisions made under uncertainty.

In situations where good probability estimates can be developed for the states of nature, the expected monetary value (EMV) method is a popular technique for making decisions. In some situations of decision making under uncertainty, the decision maker may not have the ability to assess probabilities of the various states of nature with confidence.

Technique Description

In general, three steps are involved in formulating a decision theory problem using the EMV method:

- Define the problem

- Identify alternatives that may be considered by the decision maker (feasible alternatives may be denoted by d_i)

- Identify those relevant future events that might occur and are beyond the control of the decision maker (may be denoted by s_j)

In decision theory terminology, an outcome that results from a specific decision and the occurrence of a particular state of nature is referred to as the *payoff*. $V(d_i, s_j)$ denotes the payoff associated with decision alternative, d_i, and state of nature, s_j.

By way of example, a project manager must decide which method to use for a business trip. A car trip would take 4 hours, with a 5 percent probability of delays of 1 hour or longer. A plane trip would take 3.5 hours (including travel time to and from the airport) with a 30 percent probability of delays of 2 hours or longer. In this scenario, d_i is the project manager's decision to drive. Based on expected values, the plane trip would have taken 4 hours 6 minutes [3.5 hours + (120 minutes × 0.30)]. According to expected value, the car trip should take 4 hours 3 minutes [4 hours + (60 minutes × 0.05)]. The alternative selected, s_j, is the fact that the project manager had no delays and arrived in 4 hours. Note the characteristics. The decision alternative, d_i, could be determined at any point in time. The state of nature, s_j, remained unknown until the risk had come and gone. The payoff, $V(d_i, s_j)$, is the 4-hour trip, completed successfully.

When Applicable

The EMV method applies during any project phase, although it typically would be generated at the onset of the project to identify the probabilities and relative costs associated with particular courses of action. Because decision analysis models can be portrayed as decision trees, they can be applied to network analysis. Probability-based branching in a network is an example of using decision analysis in a network analysis framework.

Input and Output

The input to the EMV method consists of the decision alternatives to be considered (what option does the project manager have), the states of nature associated with the decision alternatives (what can happen), and the probability of occurrence for each state of nature (what are the chances that a given scenario will happen). The output of the EMV method is the expected payoff values for each decision alternative under consideration.

Major Steps in Applying the Technique

The EMV criterion requires that the analyst compute the expected value for each alternative to select the alternative yielding the best expected value. Because, ultimately, only one state of nature can occur (only one given scenario can come to pass), the associated probabilities must satisfy the following condition:

$$P(s_j) \geq 0 \text{ for all states of nature}_j$$

$$\sum_{j=1}^{n} P(s_j) = P(s_1) + P(s_2) + P(s_3) + \dots + P(s_n)$$

For this equation,

$P(s_j)$ = probability of occurrence for the state of nature (s_j)

n = number of possible states of nature

The expected monetary value of a decision alternative, d_i, is derived through the following equation:

$$EMV(d_i) = \sum_{j=1}^{n} P(s_j) V(d_i, s_1)$$

In other words, the expected monetary value of a decision alternative is the product of the payoff and the probability that the payoff will occur. The probability is expressed as a percentage for each potential state of nature. If the analyst has done the analysis properly, all the probabilities will total 100 percent. The following is an example of a situation in which the EMV method can be used to make a decision.

Consider the decision of whether to purchase Acme water pumps or Nadir water pumps for a fleet of 400 trucks, based exclusively on the failure rates of the pumps, their relative maintenance cost in the first year of operation, and the purchase price. Historically, the organization has saved time, energy, and risk by replacing all water pumps in the fleet at the same time.

Acme water pumps cost $500 and have a failure rate of 5 percent in the first year of operation. Reinstalling a failed (and rebuilt) Acme pump costs $150. Maintenance on pumps that do not fail is $100 per year. Acme reimburses all maintenance costs on failed pumps.

Nadir water pumps cost only $485, but have a failure rate of 15 percent in the first year of operation. Reinstalling a failed (and rebuilt) Nadir pump costs $200. Maintenance on pumps that do not fail is $100 per year. Nadir reimburses all maintenance costs on failed pumps.

A decision table can be constructed that presents this problem with respect to two decision alternatives and the respective states of nature. Figure 15 depicts the decision table for this problem and the associated analysis.

The analyst has the option of building a table or a decision tree, or doing both, based on personal preference. The decision tree graphically represents the decision under consideration (Figure 16). Although the tree itself may never be drawn, all relevant events must be listed and analyzed to determine problems that can occur as the process reaches each decision point. Experts are consulted to identify each problem and possible resolution and to assign probabilities to the various problems and resolutions. Any realistic number of sequential resolution efforts can be evaluated.

Consider the same problem analyzed over 3 years. If failure rates and maintenance costs remain the same annually, the EMV of buying Acme would increase to only $323,000; the EMV of buying Nadir would be $332,000.

Use of Results

Given the expected monetary values of the decision alternatives, the analyst's selection of the appropriate alternative is predicated on whether the objective is to maximize profit or minimize cost. For the sample problem, because the objective was to minimize cost, the analyst would select the alternative with the lowest EMV. When the difference between decision alternatives is small, other programmatic factors may be considered when making the decision.

In the example provided, the apparent price gap between the two pumps has shrunk from $6,000 (the difference when only purchase price is considered) to $1,000 (the difference when other factors are considered). It allows the decision maker to question whether the increased quality afforded by an Acme pump is worth $1,000 to the organization.

Decision Alternatives   **States of Nature**

	Fail	Maintain
Buy Acme $d_1 = \$200{,}000$	$P(s_1) = 0.05$ 400 trucks (0.05 failure rate) ($150 per repair)	$P(s_2) = 0.95$ 400 trucks (0.95 maintenance rate) ($100 per maintenance event)
Buy Nadir $d_2 = \$194{,}000$	$P(s_1) = 0.15$ 400 trucks (0.15 failure rate) ($200 per repair)	$P(s_2) = 0.85$ 400 trucks (0.85 maintainance rate) ($100 per maintainance event)

Analysis

EMV (Buy Acme)

$200,000	400 pumps ($500 each)
3,000	400 trucks (0.05 failure rate) ($150 per repair)
38,000	400 trucks (0.95 maintenance rate) ($100 per truck)
$241,000	

EMV (Buy Nadir)

$194,000	400 trucks ($485 each)
12,000	400 trucks (0.15 failure rate) ($200 per repair)
34,000	400 trucks (0.85 maintenance rate) ($100 per truck)
$240,000	

If objective is based on a 1-year time frame and cost alone, buy Nadir.

Figure 15. Decision Table

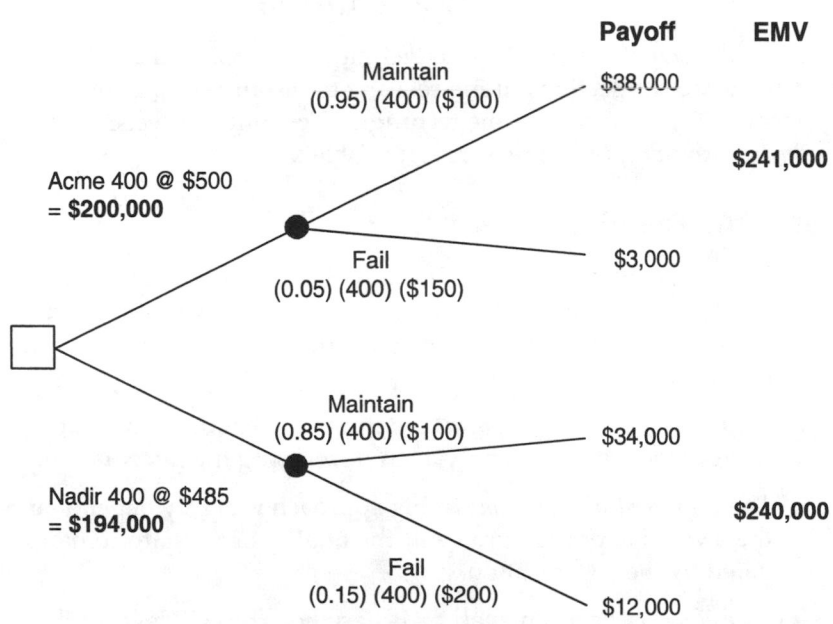

Figure 16. Decision Tree

Resource Requirements

With respect to resource requirements, the EMV technique is simplistic and can usually be calculated easily after obtaining the input to the model. As decision problems become more complex, with an increasing number of decision alternatives and states of nature, the time required to create decision tables or decision trees will also increase.

Reliability

One of the most attractive features of the EMV method of decision analysis is that after obtaining the respective input to the model, no ambiguity exists regarding the analysis. The reliability of the results is predicated on the validity of the input to the model. If analysts can define all relevant decision alternatives, states of nature, and respective probabilities realistically, the model will reflect reality.

Another significant benefit of the EMV method is that it can readily be portrayed in a diagram, making a conceptual understanding of the problem, the alternatives, and the analysis easier.

Selection Criteria

As with each of the chapters on techniques, decision analysis is assessed against selection criteria relating to resource requirements, applications, and output for the technique. To compare decision analysis with other techniques, review Table 4.

Resource Requirements

- Decision analysis *cost* includes only the time to gather the data and to conduct the analysis. A skilled analyst requires only a limited amount of time to assess the data available and to review its validity.

- *Proper facilities and equipment* are limited to enough personal computers to support analysts in developing the information.

- The *time needed to implement* this approach is highly dependent on the level of depth required and the quality of the output mandated by the organization.

- *Ease of use* in decision analysis is based on the skill level of the analyst. Comparatively speaking (when reviewed against the other techniques), this approach has a significantly shorter learning curve and thus does not require someone who has been conducting decision analyses over an extended period of time. It can be effectively taught, and because the results are quantitative, they are easier to review for flawed analyses.

- The *project manager's time commitment* to this particular technique is very limited. The project manager is normally responsible only for a final review of the output.

Applications

Decision analysis lends itself well to all the following applications.

- For *project status reporting*, decision analysis allows the project manager to provide quantitative information on future events. Because few techniques provide that information, decision analysis provides a valuable piece of information essential to quality risk management.

- *Major planning decisions* should hinge on the potential for success. Because decision analysis reviews potential for success, assigning it probability and expected monetary value, it is invaluable.

- *Contract strategy selection* is keyed to the potential success of the buyer, vendor, contractor, or subcontractor involved. Because contracts are often driven by monetary decisions, EMV and decision trees can help determine whether the contract strategy is appropriate to the value of the contract.

- As with contract strategy selection, *milestone preparation* is most often a step conducted at the beginning of the project. Here, decision analysis has limited utility, unless it is applied to the schedules to determine the potential for success in terms of the schedule. If the milestones are budget driven, decision analysis becomes even more appropriate.

- *Design guidance* can stem directly from decision analysis, because various designs will have different implications in terms of the potential for profits and the potential for technical success.

- In *source selection*, decision analysis applies if there is a history or data record for the vendors under consideration. If that information is available, decision analysis can be effectively applied. Often, such evidence is primarily anecdotal and, as such, does not work well with this technique.

- *Budget submittal* may be directly affected by decision analysis, because some organizations use decision analysis as part of the consideration for budget allocations.

Output

The output from decision analysis can be extraordinarily helpful. It may also be useless. The critical value in terms of the output is the quality of the input.

- *Accuracy* is highly analyst and data dependent. If the project can be modeled accurately, the output will be accurate. The inverse is also true. To generate effective, accurate information, the data must come from a valid, reliable source and must be analyzed by someone who clearly understands the implications of the technique.

- The *level of detail* is predicated on what the project manager deems necessary. Decision analysis is fully scalable. It can be conducted at the broad-scale and detailed levels. As such, it offers an advantage over techniques that can be applied only at one end of the range.

- The *utility* of decision analysis is not as high as many other techniques, because it does not provide the same diversity of output or address the myriad questions that other techniques do. Instead, it works best when it provides intense focus on a single issue.

Summary

Decision analysis affords project managers a multiperspective analysis on a single issue. It does not answer broad, far-reaching project management questions. Instead, it draws on specifics to paint the nuances of the larger picture. Decision analysis also gives the project manager some quantitative information to present in case of any significant conflict. If decision analysis is used to analyze the right questions using the right input, it can become a powerful tool for the project manager. The keys to making decision analysis effective are to use the tools properly and to ensure that the information being analyzed is current, valid, and accurate.

Chapter 9

ESTIMATING RELATIONSHIPS

The estimating relationship method enables project personnel to evaluate a project and, based on that evaluation, use an equation to determine an appropriate contingency or risk funds budget. When using this method, the contingency funds represent the amount of funding, above that determined by cost analysis alone, required for work associated with unanticipated risks. The contingency funds requirement computed is usually expressed as a percentage of the baseline cost estimate. The technique is called an estimating relationship method because it uses some of the same techniques associated with cost estimating relationships (CERs) used in parametric cost estimating.

Technique Description

The CER method is based on the observation that costs of systems seem to correlate with design or performance variables. The independent variables, often called explanatory variables, are analyzed using regression analysis to describe the underlying mechanism relating such variables to cost. This approach to cost estimating is widely accepted and easy to apply, even for complex functions.

This ease of application makes it natural to use the same techniques to estimate costs resulting from risks. The approach attempts to discover which project characteristics can be refined into discrete variables that can then be correlated with the historically demonstrated need for contingency or risk funds. Regression analysis using actual contingency funds from past projects, expressed as a percentage of total costs, is performed to develop an equation with which to estimate contingency fund requirements for a new project not in a database.

The application of this technique is described in "Major Steps in Applying the Technique." In an example describing this application, project personnel evaluate four project and subcontractor characteristics known to affect the level of uncertainty. Each characteristic is assigned a value based on a scale provided for that characteristic. For this example, the four characteristics and their values are engineering complexity (0 to 5), organizational proficiency/experience (0 to 3), degree of system definition (0 to 3), and multiple users (0 or 1). The sum of these numerics is entered as the value X in an estimating equation like the following:*

$$y = \left(0.192 - 0.337X + 0.009X^2\right) \times 100$$

This formula (derived from years of experience in a specific environment) determines the percentage contingency fund requirement, y. The model shown in this example is usable only for X values between 2 and 12. Lower values indicate essentially no need for contingency funds.

When Applicable

This method of estimating the additional funding needed to cover anticipated risks has limited application. It can be used only if the research has already been done to establish a valid historical relationship between the key project characteristics or contract characteristics of similar projects and contingency fund requirements.** The method is most applicable in circumstances in which good historical project description and contingency fund requirements are available for several similar projects. If the required risk funding estimating relationship is available, this method has the advantage of being both quick and easy to apply.

---

* The numbers in this formula were derived in the U.S. Department of Defense environment by the Defense Systems Management College. As such, they may or may not be appropriate within your organization. They are based on the collective experience of the organization and the implications of those specific characteristics within their project environments.

** In this case, the research was done at the U.S. Air Force Electronics Systems Division.

Input and Output

The input for an estimating relationship model, such as the equation in "Technique Description," consists of judgment values characterizing the four project or contract factors described in the example.

Regarding output, the estimating relationship method provides a percentage that is applied to the estimated baseline cost to determine the amount of total or contract contingency funds required. This percentage value is computed using an equation similar to that used in the example, with the X value being the sum of the four factor values determined by project personnel.

Major Steps in Applying the Technique

Assuming that an appropriate contingency estimating equation is not available, the first step in using this method is by far the most difficult. The first step is to develop an equation relating project characteristics to contingency fund requirements. The most difficult part of this step is finding valid historical characteristics and contingency fund data for enough similar projects to carry out regression analysis. Data from at least 10 past projects should be used to develop an estimating relationship equation.

The second part of this step is to determine the project or contract characteristics that drive contingency fund requirements and for which historical data have been collected. After the historical data have been collected, using regression analysis to identify these characteristics is relatively simple. The summing of judgment values for each of the four project characteristics, as done in the previous example, is only one way to develop one or more independent variables for an estimating relationship for contingency fund requirements. Geometric mean or weighted average techniques could also be used. Multiple regression analysis techniques frequently are used for parametric cost estimating.

The final step is to use the prediction equation derived through extensive analysis of past projects (coupled with the current project characteristic information) to compute a percentage for the contingency funds needed to cover anticipated additional costs associated with risk. It may be useful to vary the project description characteristic data somewhat and recompute the estimating equation to assess the impact of such changes on the computed contingency requirements. This sensitivity analysis is usually prudent because of the uncertainty associated with the predicted project or contract characteristics.

Use of Results

To cover funds needed for risk, a percentage of the estimated contract or project cost is added to the basic cost estimate. For example, if the contract cost estimate was $100 million and the prediction equation provided a result of 20 percent, $20 million would be added for risk, making the total estimated contract cost $120 million.

Resource Requirements

After a suitable contingency fund requirement prediction equation is available, only a few hours are required to apply this method. Most of the effort required involves interviewing project personnel to obtain their judgments on the contract or project characteristic values to be used. If a prediction equation has to be developed, 1 to 3 months of a skilled analyst's time would be required, depending on the difficulty in acquiring the needed data. If the required data are not available, it becomes impossible to produce a satisfactory prediction equation.

Reliability

When applied, this method provides results that significantly increase cost estimates (based primarily on extrapolating historical data that may include costs for risks that have been experienced already) to allow for risk. Because the additional funds are based primarily on judgment values, they are subject to question. If this technique is to be used, it would always be prudent for the project manager to have the method (including the prediction equation to be used) reviewed and approved by upper management before using it as the basis for a viable request for additional funds to cover risks. The method can be used only where adequate historical data are available to develop a sound contingency fund requirement prediction equation.

Selection Criteria

As with each of the chapters on techniques, estimating relationships is reviewed against selection criteria relating to resource requirements, applications, and output for the technique. To compare estimating relationships with other techniques, review Table 4.

Resource Requirements

- The *cost* of the estimating relationship technique hinges largely on the existence of the availability of a parametric cost model specifically designed to estimate contingency reserve or risk funds as a function of one or more project parameters. If such a model is not available, 1 to 3 resource-months may be required to develop it. If the required historical data are not available, developing the required cost model may be impossible. If a satisfactory model is available, it generally takes only a few days to use it.

- *Proper facilities and equipment* relate primarily to the databases with the appropriate information and the tools themselves. Otherwise, very little equipment is required. The model equations are usually so simple that a hand-held calculator can be used to compute required contingency reserve fund requirements.

- The *time needed to implement* the technique can range from a matter of days to as long as 3 months, depending on the maturity of the organization in terms of the technique. If the technique has been developed and exercised regularly, then only a few days will be required. Otherwise, a 1- to 3-month window is required to develop the appropriate information.

- Estimating relationships have high *ease of use*, because after they are built, they require only the appropriate calculations to be developed. Ease of use after the models are constructed becomes a function of ease in data gathering.

- The *project manager's time commitment* is extremely limited, but there are some responsibilities for the project manager. The project manager must support the technique's use so that key project personnel will provide the cost analyst with time judgments or information needed as input for the model.

Applications

- *Project status reporting* is not supported well by this technique. It is far more effective as a tool at project inception, rather than at project midpoints.

- The only *major planning decision* supported by the technique is determining the extent of contingency reserve or risk funds to be included in the initial budget request or baseline budget.

- The *contract strategy selection* may hinge in small part on the level of risk funding required for the project. Otherwise, there is no relationship between the technique and this application.

- *Milestone preparation* and *design guidance* are not supported by this technique.

- *Source selection* may be a crucial input to the technique, but it is not supported by the estimating relationship output.

- *Budget submittal* is the primary application for this technique. By computing the level of contingency reserve or risk funds required, the project manager can develop a budget that incorporates and reflects risk issues and allows for the vagaries of real-world project management.

Output

- The *accuracy* of the technique is considered low, primarily because the historical databases on which such models are based are small. The accuracy also comes into question because accurately defining what funds were spent to address risk on past projects is often difficult.

- This method provides a *level of detail* that is unacceptable to the detail-oriented analyst. It provides little or no information with respect to which parts of the project are riskier and, therefore, more likely to require additional funding.

- Because so few models of this type are available, and even their uses are subject to question, the overall *utility* of this method must be considered low.

Summary

The estimating relationship method is not well understood by many project managers. Some survey respondents indicated that they had used this technique when they had really used parametric cost estimating methods for some or all the project cost estimates. Such analysis is more accurately described as all or part of a life-cycle cost analysis. The estimating relationship method is defined by the use of parametric estimating methods to estimate risk or contingency reserve fund requirements. Currently, few parametric cost models are available with which to do this.

Chapter 10

NETWORK ANALYSIS

A quality schedule, essentially an objective-oriented plan of action, is critical for effective project planning, implementation, and control. It includes activities and events that must be accomplished to achieve the desired objectives. Many project managers are familiar with the concept of network-based scheduling in project management. Network-based schedules formalize the scheduling process and result in a graphic that displays not only the activities that must be accomplished but also relationships among the activities (which activities precede, succeed, or are parallel to other activities). The utility of network diagramming in general includes the following:

- Focuses the attention of all management levels during the planning phase

- Estimates project completion date

- Displays the scope of the project

- Assesses resource requirements

- Facilitates what-if exercises

- Highlights critical activities

- Evaluates performance

The following actions are keys to successful network development:

- Determine appropriate level of detail (such as aggregate, intermediate)

- Identify relevant activities

- Define relationships among activities (such as dependence, concurrence)

- Forecast time durations

- Involve all individuals relevant to the preceding

In many situations, project managers assume responsibility for planning, scheduling, and controlling projects that consist of numerous separate jobs or tasks performed by a variety of departments, project offices, and individuals. Often, these projects are so complex or large that the project manager cannot possibly remember all the information pertaining to the plan, schedule, and progress of the project.

In these situations, the Program Evaluation and Review Technique (PERT) and critical path method (CPM) have proven to be extremely valuable in helping project managers carry out their management responsibilities. Besides being one of the original scheduling techniques, PERT (developed during the Polaris submarine program in the late 1950s) was also the first significant project-oriented risk analysis tool. The objectives of PERT were to manage schedule risk by establishing the shortest development schedule, to monitor project progress, and to fund or apply necessary resources to maintain the schedule. Figure 17 represents a PERT network.

A significant output of a network analysis is identifying the critical path, which consists of those activities that must be finished on time or the project will be delayed. Activities in the critical path compose the longest single path through the network. Their total duration represents the project duration. Most modern project management software highlights the critical path activities for each identification. Although this helps identify some higher-risk activities, it also identifies those activities with free time, or slack. Activities not on the critical path can afford some modest schedule slippage without affecting the overall project schedule.

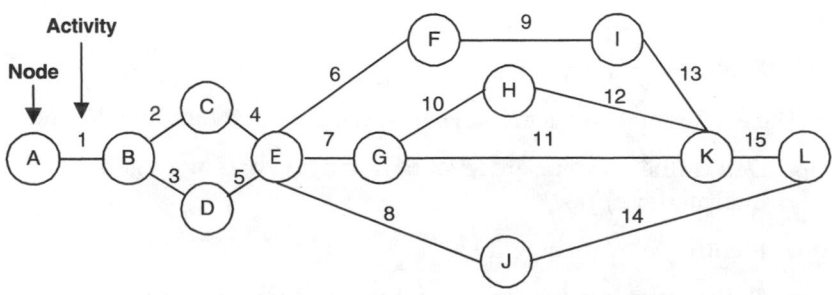

Figure 17. Project Represented As a Network

Technique Description

The original networking technique was based on the arrow diagramming method (ADM) or activity-on-arrow method of representing logical relationships between activities. ADM represents all predecessor and successor activities as finish-to-start relationships. Successor activities are not initiated until the predecessor is complete. However, because this form of relationship is not always true for predecessor/successor activities, other networking methodologies were developed to reflect the realities of those dependencies more accurately. Newer computer-based networking systems use the precedence diagramming method (PDM) or activity-on-node diagram to represent network logic. PDM allows greater flexibility than ADM in describing predecessor/successor relationships. With PDM, the following relationships can be described in addition to the finish-to-start relationship:

- *Finish-to-finish:* Successor activity cannot finish until after the predecessor has been completed

- *Start-to-start:* Successor activity cannot start until after the predecessor has started

- *Start-to-finish:* Successor activity cannot be completed until the predecessor has started

Newer network-based risk models also use PDM. The description that follows is based on the PDM networks, because they have become more popular as both scheduling and risk tools.

To reflect the realities of risk-related issues accurately, network diagrams have been enhanced over the years. Logic has been added to increase the functionality of network analysis as a risk analysis tool. In probability-based networks, uncertainty manifests itself in two ways. First, activities may have uncertain outcomes for to complete, cost to complete, or achievement of some technical level of performance. Generally, technical performance is a fixed parameter, while time and cost vary. Second, initiating successors with a common predecessor may be predictable only against the probability of the predecessor's success. For example, a test outcome (pass/fail) may determine whether the next activity is a progressive continuation of a plan or a corrective action. Because the outcome cannot be predicted with certainty, it is driven by probability. The network model (using tools like Scitor's Process Charter for iterative, probability-based cycles) can assign the level of unpredictability by ascribing a specific percentage to the probability of either outcome. This allows the analyst to work through the model repeatedly to determine relevant probabilities of completing within time or cost constraints or of meeting performance levels.

As previously mentioned, proper network development is based on selecting the appropriate level of detail. The consensus is that a broad view should be accomplished before attempting to model the details of the project structure. Aggregate-level networks will provide a more realistic determination of what detail-level networks will contain. However, aggregate-level networks will also contain more inherent uncertainty than would be the case at a finer level of detail. As project requirements and information become more readily available, network models will evolve to a greater level of detail.

When Applicable

Networks are formulated based on project activities, interrelationships among activities, and constraints (time, money, human resources, technology, and so on). Because all projects have these characteristics, network analysis applies universally. Using the technique is easier if network-based project schedules already exist, because analysts can then make logic modifications so that network data can be incorporated readily into a risk analysis software program. If a network does not already exist, one must be created. The time saved transforming an existing network rather than creating one provides a strong argument for network-based project scheduling from the beginning of a project.

Input and Output

The input for the development of the network risk model consists of probability density functions. (Chapter 4 and Appendix D discuss some techniques available for quantifying expert judgment.) Initially, input to the network model may be qualitative judgment that must be transformed into quantitative information. Thus, it is imperative that all individuals who fulfill a relevant project role provide input during the development process. Their contributions affect the credibility of the resulting network. Standard output from network risk models includes probability curves; bar charts comparing baseline and "risk-free" schedules; cost histograms; cumulative density functions (CDFs); and the mean, standard deviation of the sample, coefficient of variation, and mode for all specified decision points and activities. These result from performing a Monte Carlo simulation of the network.

Most packages also produce a criticality index for each activity. This index shows how often each activity appeared on the critical path during the course of the simulation process. Cost curves and histograms can also be produced that may indicate the direction the project is taking. This information can be used to continually adjust labor, material, and time estimates.

Major Steps in Applying the Technique

The first step in this modeling process is for the analyst to develop a rough-cut network manually. To develop a realistic model of the project, the analyst must identify all relevant parameters, such as activities, relationships, and probabilities. As previously stated, all relevant project personnel should participate in developing and validating the network.

After the rough-cut network is developed, the analyst can enter the information into a computer for evaluation. Various software packages are currently available for network risk analysis. The tools are generally available for integration with modern project management software to facilitate evaluating networks in the greater context of the project plan. Monte Carlo analyses can be conducted with many of these software packages. Typically, 1,000 to 6,000 simulations are processed on a large-scale project. These simulations result in a statistically calculated scenario that predicts the eventual course of the project with a confidence level as specified by the user.

Use of Results

The output of this technique process is extremely useful to the project manager. The performance of network risk analysis generally provides an in-depth understanding of the sources and degree of risks. Results of the risk analysis process provide the information required to execute the risk response control phase of risk management effectively.

Resource Requirements

Because most network risk assessments are carried out by the project team, costs should be estimated from human resource requirements. A comprehensive network analysis for a major project may require definition of between 200 and 1,000 activities and also weeks of preparation, information gathering, and expert interviews to establish probability density functions (PDFs) and build the network. Obtaining the information required to construct the network generally entails more time and rechecking than initially might seem necessary. This is because the project plan usually undergoes continual revision and definition and the support team may not fully understand relationships among project activities.

Although the difficulty and time required for network definition can pose a problem, the effort of constructing a consistent and acceptable network model forces the responsible participants to plan effectively and to understand how their own segments of the project fit into the whole. Project managers have indicated that this benefit alone can justify all the effort in accomplishing a formal network risk assessment.

Reliability

The reliability of network risk analysis is a function of multiple factors. Developing a network that accurately reflects activities and relationships among activities is crucial to the resulting network analysis. Thus, it is imperative that all relevant project personnel provide input to developing and modifying the network. Defining PDFs for the cost, schedule, and performance aspects of the project is also of fundamental importance. Because the Monte Carlo simulations that predict the course of the project are based on the respective PDFs, accuracy of the PDFs in describing the cost, schedule, and performance parameters of the project is critical for a reliable analysis. The more reliable the network developed, the more reliable the analysis will be.

Selection Criteria

As with each of the chapters on techniques, network analysis is reviewed against selection criteria relating to resource requirements, applications, and output for the technique. To compare network analysis with other techniques, review Table 4.

Resource Requirements

- The *cost* of network analysis depends largely on whether the networks are already developed for the project. If so, they can be used for the risk models, and extensive labor can be saved.

- *Proper facilities and equipment* should include reasonably sophisticated personal computers loaded with current project management software, coupled with plotters or large-form printers. Without this equipment, the techniques may bog down as massive cut-and-paste operations, with team members developing giant networks by taping together dozens of small sheets of paper.

- The *time needed to implement* the technique can be extensive, because there is a significant learning curve associated with using the more complex aspects of the tools.

- Network analysis has a low *ease of use*, because the processes of building the networks, capturing expert judgment, and understanding the software are not easy to master.

- Although the *project manager's time commitment* is slight to moderate, the project team must be convinced of the manager's commitment to the task.

Applications

Networks have a high degree of utility, as discussed earlier in this chapter; therefore all applications listed are relevant.

- *Project status reporting* is clearly supported by network analysis, because changes in the duration of activities as the project progresses may drive changes in the project critical path.

- *Major planning decisions* should include a review of the network diagrams and the network risk diagrams. Because even modest changes in the network can have significant implications, all major planning decisions should be reviewed in the context of a thorough network analysis.

- Network analysis supports *contract strategy selection,* because the flexibility of the schedule may make certain types of clauses (especially liquidated damages) either more or less acceptable.

- Because milestones often become focal points in a network, network analysis becomes a critical input to *milestone preparation.*

- For *design guidance,* network analysis serves a role in clarifying the schedule risks and the overall implications of switching from one design to another.

- *Source selection* may in part be driven by scheduling considerations. Thus, network analysis is important here as well.

- *Budget submittal* is probably the least applicable category for network analysis, although budgets are often driven by resource loading, and if the resources are assigned across a longer period of time, budgets will inherently be higher. Thus, there is even a modest relationship between budget submittals and network analyses.

Output

With respect to output, the accuracy of the analysis is a function of the validity of the network itself and the levels of effort generated for each activity.

- The *accuracy* of the analysis is a direct function of the validity of the network itself and the level of effort generated for each activity. If there is a significant (perhaps disproportionate) level of effort in a single activity, the accuracy of the network can be diminished. If the work packages are developed in a relatively even fashion (similar sizes, similar costs, similar durations), there is a higher probability of accuracy.

- The *level of detail* is determined by management in many cases, or by the project manager, so it can be low, medium, or high. Different project managers use network analysis to achieve different perspectives, so the level of detail is a function of the level of detail desired.

- The *utility* of the networks generally is high, if for no other reason than the fact that managers are forced to fuse detail into their plans before project implementation.

Summary

Network analyses are critical to risk management, given their critical role in ensuring that schedule objectives are met. These analyses focus attention on the relationships of activities and the interrelationships of risk among those activities. Although the network analysis models sometimes fail to give cost risk its due, they are invaluable early in the project when schedule risk is the greatest. As with most tools, they are not the only tool required to evaluate or mitigate risk comprehensively. However, when used with other tools and techniques, network analyses are invaluable to the risk manager.

Chapter 11

LIFE-CYCLE COST ANALYSIS

One survey of project managers indicated that they viewed funding cuts as the source of risk having the greatest effect in implementing major projects. To control such risks, a project manager must be able to quickly determine potential cost implications of new information (such as funding constraints pertinent to the project). Other new information affecting project costs may include test failures, schedule slips, and production rate reductions. The project manager must have quick access to potential cost implications of some of the choices to be made as the project progresses. Many projects meet such needs with a computerized life-cycle cost (LCC) model. These models are sometimes called quick reaction cost models or quick reaction models. Such models can be useful for cost estimating, trade-off analysis, production rate and quantity analysis, warranty analysis, sensitivity analysis, and logistics support studies.

Technique Description

The LCC technique consists of using a series of equations to analyze project costs based on product and project information. However, it will vary from model to model and may vary significantly from project to project, depending on the nature of the project and its status. An important aspect of an LCC model is that, given some informed input, the model can be run quickly and provide not only a new total LCC estimate but also some insight regarding where costs are likely to change. The model equations usually are developed based on logic and experience on similar past projects.

Cost elements of LCC models vary significantly. However, where applicable, they usually include development, production, and the full spectrum of extended operating and support costs. The exact nature of product and project information is addressed in "Input and Output."

When Applicable

Use of an LCC model is applicable whenever a manager needs a quick estimate of the cost implications of a past or pending event. However, the timely development of useful cost estimates depends totally on having a completed and tested LCC model available for immediate use. Such a model is very applicable to situations in which budget cuts are proposed by upper management and the project manager has only a short time to describe the effect of such cuts.

Input and Output

Most LCC models have extensive input that varies from model to model. Timely use of these models dictates that input values be maintained continually so that only those that would change because of recent or pending actions must be obtained to carry out the desired cost analysis. This is especially important when using detailed LCC models that aggregate costs based on the characteristics of many individual subsystems and line replaceable units. Important input values common to many LCC models include the following:

- Production quantity by year
- Development test quantities
- Cost quantity curve slopes
- Support equipment requirements
- Number of facilities to which the deliverable will be deployed
- Spare and replacement part requirements
- Nonrecurring production costs
- Deployment life of the system
- Planned utilization rate
- Failure rates

The output for LCC models is as varied as the models themselves. No matter what output is selected, one should be an overall summary of the total LCCs broken down by when funds will actually be allocated. Other useful output options include total LCC breakouts by year, cost element, equipment component, or combinations thereof. Output values may be in fixed and specified base-year monetary values or, if inflation rates were provided in the input, in monetary values inflated to the year in which they must be allocated.

Major Steps in Applying the Technique

The first step is to develop a model tailored to the nature of the project and anticipated cost information needs. Without this key step, timely estimates cannot be generated. Developing such a model and gathering the required input values usually requires significant resource commitment. However, this effort can often be reduced greatly by tailoring an LCC model already used for a similar system.

The second step is to use the LCC model to address a specific issue. This may require data collection, but that effort should be significantly less than the effort to develop the model. If a model is already available and programmed on a computer, gathering input data is almost always the largest part of the effort to prepare an LCC estimate.

The last step is to review the model output, ensure that results are reasonable, and address any questions. An LCC analysis might involve computation and comparison of several estimates. The model is only an abstraction of the real world. Therefore, decision makers often demand and generally appreciate logical arguments that tend to substantiate the model's numerical results. Models often provide sensitivity analysis using a range of input values around the primary input values to see how changes affect the model's computed LCC estimates.

Use of Results

LCC analysis results can be used to assess costs and, thereby, cost risks associated with critical decisions. LCC models can be used to develop or carry out the following:

- LCC estimates
- Production rate and quantity analyses
- Design trade-off analyses
- Cost-driver sensitivity analyses
- Resource projections
- Repair-level analyses
- Warranty analyses
- Reliability growth analyses
- Operational availability analyses

Resource Requirements

Development, programming, and testing of a tailored LCC model could require 6 to 12 months of a research analyst's time. The analyst may need to be a skilled accounting professional, familiar with the organization and its projects. However, this time can be reduced significantly if an existing LCC model can be modified to the project's needs. Although LCC models normally exist within an organization, they are often buried within functional departments and are not readily available to project management staff. Before launching an effort to develop any LCC model, the status of existing models within the organization should be evaluated.

Reliability

LCC model analysis is relatively common in extremely large organizations, especially government, and is widely accepted as a quantitative basis for decision making. It may enhance the credibility of a project manager's analysis (from an upper management perspective) if a model that has already gained acceptance within the organization is selected. The project manager should determine whether such a model is available. All models have the limitation that input data values must reflect significant and true differences among alternatives if the model is to produce valid and useful LCC differences as different implementation alternatives and risk alternatives are analyzed.

Selection Criteria

As with each of the chapters on techniques, life-cycle cost analysis is reviewed against selection criteria relating to resource requirements, applications, and output for the technique. To compare life-cycle cost analysis with other techniques, review Table 4.

Resource Requirements

- The *cost* associated with LCC analysis is relatively low if a model is already available. The most expensive component of the analysis is generally input data collection, which normally is derived from a variety of sources. If a project-specific model must be developed, the resource requirements to do this can be reduced greatly if a demonstrated model for a similar system can be tailored to the project.

- *Proper facilities and equipment* normally consist of a personal computer, which today has adequate memory, storage, and application development capabilities to handle even the most complex LCC models.

- The *time needed to implement* the model is just slightly longer than the time required to gather the data. The greater the volume of data required to support the model, the greater the time involved.

- There is high *ease of use* in performing an LCC analysis, even one involving many estimates for different scenarios or sets of assumptions, if the model is available.

- The *project manager's time commitment* is determined by whether he or she is the only team member skilled in applying the technique. If so, the commitment will be high, because the data gatherers and computer data entry must be overseen by the project manager. If a skilled analyst is available, the time commitment is minimized.

Applications

Because cost is an important management consideration, the results of LCC analysis apply to many project decisions and may involve multiple projects across an organization. After this capability is developed, it has significant value whenever a quick assessment is needed. That assessment normally captures the cost implications of design, production rate, and other project changes.

- *Project status reporting* is supported by LCC only if the model includes criteria for projects in progress. If the model is designed exclusively for projects at inception, it may be inappropriate to use the models to assess the projected LCC at midproject.

- *Major planning decisions,* particularly those at project inception, may be driven by this technique's output. Thus, there is a close match between LCC analysis and early major planning decisions.

- *Contract strategy selection* is often driven by budgetary concerns, which are the province of LCC analysis.

- There is little true correlation between LCC analysis and *milestone preparation,* unless the milestones developed have a budgetary (rather than schedule) focus.

- *Design guidance* can be readily supported by LCC analysis, because the life-cycle costs of two different designs will almost always be significantly different. By evaluating designs from a life-cycle perspective, this technique provides a valuable tool in determining the value and validity of a given design option.

- *Source selection* can have a profound effect on life-cycle costs, which means that selection approaches and results are key input to the analysis. Conversely, the tool can assess the long-term implications of one vendor versus another. Thus, the tool supports the application, and the application supports the tool.

- *Budget submittal* is often more than one set of numbers presented to management. It is often a set of options available for management's consideration. LCC analysis affords long-term perspectives on various options, rather than the conventional, short-term view. This additional perspective may rationalize numerous specific actions that may, on the surface, appear counterproductive.

Output

- The *accuracy* of LCC analysis is medium. Usually, such estimates can be improved if significantly more time is taken to have the project team take a more detailed look at how changes would affect a project. LCC analysis is better for analyzing differences among alternatives than for accurately predicting future costs.

- Depending on the specific LCC model, the analysis output can provide a considerable *level of detail* regarding where cost might change as the result of project changes. By comparing these critical points in various analyses, it gives the project manager a greater volume of decision-making data.

- The overall *utility* of LCC analysis is high because it provides timely insight relative to a wide range of management decisions.

Summary

LCC analysis has been used widely over the years as a result of growing concern about rapidly increasing operating and support costs. Because economic considerations are an integral part of projects, LCC can be an important design or early development consideration. Both project-specific and general-purpose LCC models can be used. The availability and familiarity of spreadsheet applications has greatly facilitated the development and use of LCC models by project personnel.

Chapter 12

COST RISK/WBS
SIMULATION MODEL

This technique takes cost risk into account not just for individual activities, but for the entire project. In many cases, there is a temptation to assume that all the project risks must be accounted for in the worst case. This technique takes a more wholistic approach. The total project cost risk is usually expressed as a cumulative probability distribution of total project cost. Such distribution information can be used to reflect project risk by computing the probability that the project can be completed for a specific monetary value or less. It can also be used to assess what level of funding would be required to virtually guarantee success (in terms of the cost parameters).

A computer is necessary to use this technique, because the analysis requires many repeated computations. Some of the software packages (for example, Risk+ and @Risk) can conduct cost analyses in addition to the network analyses mentioned in Chapter 10. However, the network models usually require significantly more input data than do pure cost risk/WBS simulation models.

Technique Description

This technique uses the Monte Carlo simulation analysis method. However, variations of the technique use other probability distributions to describe the cost risk associated with each WBS cost element.

Uniform, triangular, beta, and other probability distributions have been used for this purpose. Use of uniform and triangular distributions makes computation easier. However, use of beta distributions allows the user more freedom in describing WBS cost element uncertainty. The different cost risk analysis approaches differ in the amount of data they require for each WBS cost element. They also differ in terms of the format used to present analysis results and assumptions with respect to the interdependence among WBS element costs.

The cost risk/WBS simulation model uses a random-number generator to simulate the uncertainty for individual WBS elements. After costs are simulated for each WBS element, they are aggregated to get a total project cost estimate. This process is repeated many times. Each time a new set of WBS element costs is developed, it is referred to as an *experiment*. The results of many such experiments provide a frequency distribution of total costs, reflecting the aggregate of the cost risks associated with all the individual WBS elements.

When Applicable

This technique applies when the project manager needs to know the probability that a project can be completed successfully at a given funding level. It also applies when there is a need to know what funding level is required to achieve a specified probability of completing a project. To ensure that this technique can be applied, the project manager must obtain sound estimates of the cost uncertainty associated with each WBS element. When a cost estimate broken out by a WBS is already available, this is a relatively quick analytical procedure to use.

Input and Output

With this analysis technique, input and output vary depending on the models used. As an example of input and output information, *Risk+* can apply various types of cost uncertainty against each individual WBS element and then generate a variety of information types.

For each model run, three elements of data are required once:

- Project name
- Monte Carlo sample size (number of iterations)
- Decision to computer either a partial analysis or completion analysis

For each WBS cost element constituting part of the total project cost estimate, five elements of data are required:

- Point-cost estimate (most likely)
- Low end of cost range value (expressed as a monetary value)

- High end of cost range value (expressed as a monetary value)

- Type of distribution curve to be applied (fixed, normal, triangular, beta, or uniform)

- Probabilities to be assigned to the curve

In Figure 18, roughly 32 of the samples fall into the range near $122,388 (the mean). That type of information is used to develop both the probability curve and the histogram. Each bar on the histogram represents a range of roughly $5,000. As you can tell by examining the histogram, the odds of project costs coming within the lowest $15,000 (the first three bars) of the range is about 10 percent.

These data can now be used to provide confidence levels based on project costs to establish adequate levels of funding. Based on Figure 18, funding would have to be set at more than $130,000 to achieve 95 percent confidence that the project would be funded adequately. That does *not* mean the project will cost $130,000. It means that, based on the simulation, there is a 95 percent probability that the project can be completed for $130,803 or less.

Major Steps in Applying the Technique

The first step in applying this type of technique is to obtain and become familiar with one of the computer programs used to implement it. It is helpful to review the guidance provided with the program to ensure that it will generate the desired output. It is rarely practical or desirable to create such a computer program.

The second step is to obtain the input data required by the model. This step is greatly facilitated if a total project cost estimate is already available, particularly if the estimate is built from the work package level of the WBS. If such estimates are available, the required WBS cost element uncertainty input data generally can be obtained by interviewing project personnel. If possible, historical cost data should be reviewed to get a sense of the range of similar WBS cost values on other projects.

The third step is to feed the input data into the model and to run it. This is generally far less time consuming than gathering the input data.

Date: 8/30/97 11:08:38 a.m.
Number of samples: 100
Unique ID: 1
Name: task 1

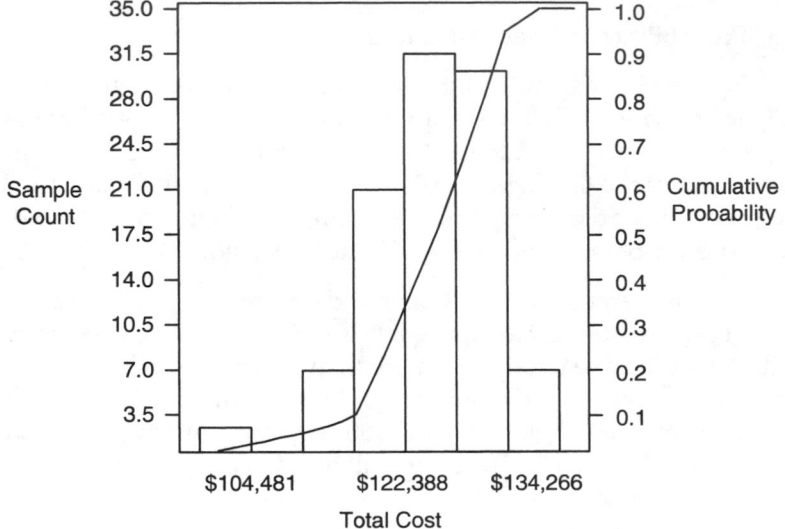

Cost standard deviation: $5,986
95% confidence interval: $1,173
Each bar represents $5,000

Cost Probability Table

Prob	Cost ($)	Prob	Cost ($)
0.05	111,542	0.55	123,953
0.10	114,121	0.60	124,510
0.15	115,638	0.65	125,158
0.20	117,606	0.70	126,421
0.25	118,802	0.75	126,773
0.30	119,438	0.80	127,602
0.35	120,204	0.85	128,476
0.40	120,870	0.90	129,682
0.45	121,520	0.95	130,803
0.50	122,568	1.00	134,266

Figure 18. Cost Risk/WBS Simulation Model

The last step is to examine output results in a cursory analysis:

- Do they appear reasonable?
- Do they provide the information required?
- Do they reflect the individual WBS element risks in the greater project context?

Use of Results

WBS simulation model results are used to show how WBS element risks may cause total project costs to vary from the point estimate used for budgets and other purposes. The results can also be used to compute estimated costs for several projects at a specified confidence level, such as 90 percent. Upper management may ask to see such information as part of the normal review process.

Resource Requirements

The primary resource requirement is a copy of a computer program using this method and the associated user guidance. Anyone with a fundamental understanding of computers and the basic input required can quickly learn to run such a model, if supported by project team members in providing WBS cost element uncertainty range and level judgments. Tools available include both stand-alone applications and those that run in tandem with project management software applications.

Reliability

The mathematics and logic of the cost risk/WBS simulation technique are basically sound. However, these models generally do not fully address the interactions between WBS elements. They usually assume either total dependence or total independence among WBS elements, but the true situation will probably vary from project to project and will almost always be somewhere in between. As such, project managers cannot expect the cost values provided by the model to reflect all the risks associated with such dynamic elements as schedule, performance, and the business environment. Given the dynamic nature of projects, the data input is frequently provided by individuals with less-than-total familiarity with the project and its risks.

Difficulty in obtaining sound and supportable input values is the greatest limit to this method.

Selection Criteria

As with each of the chapters on techniques, the cost risk/WBS simulation model is reviewed against selection criteria relating to resource requirements, applications, and output for the technique. To compare the cost risk/WBS simulation model with other techniques, review Table 4.

Resource Requirements

- The *cost* associated with this technique includes both the one-time cost of software acquisition (which can range from several hundred to several thousand dollars) and the cost for a resource to gather the data and develop the appropriate scenario to run through the computer.

- As to whether the *proper facilities and equipment* are available, the answer in many organizations is no. Although the investment is a one-time experience, some organizations feel that the information delivered through the tool is data overkill.

- The *time needed to implement* after the tools and skills are in place is, much as with estimating relationships (Chapter 9), in proportion to the time required to gather the necessary data.

- The *ease of use* associated with this analysis method is high after a few hours of hands-on experience. Available programs come with instructions. The real challenge is associated with obtaining and substantiating sound values for all the cost element uncertainty information. Ideally, the best source for such information would be past experience on similar projects, but that type of information is rarely available.

- The *project manager's time commitment* is slight but necessary to ensure that team members provide this information in a timely manner.

Applications

- *Project status reporting* represents only a small fraction of the overall use of the technique. Only one respondent to a major survey conducted by the Defense Systems Management College identified using this technique for this purpose. Even so, as the tools become more inexpensive and user-friendly, the application here could readily increase.

- The cost risk/WBS simulation model is best applied as *major planning decisions* are made. The model provides insight into the range of possibilities associated with any given modification to the plan.

- *Contract strategy selection* and *milestone preparation* are not applications that can effectively use the cost risk/WBS simulation model.

- This technique can be applied in *design guidance* if the range of cost implications is required for a variety of different designs.

- *Source selection* is not a common application, but the cost risk/WBS simulation model has been applied to examine the cost range for different potential vendors, based on their submitted costs and WBSs.

- *Budget submittal* is also a rare use for this technique, although the cost risk/WBS simulation model will provide management with clear insight into the best case, worst case, and most likely cost parameters for the project.

Output

- The *accuracy* of output results is limited by the subjective nature of most of the input data used to conduct the analysis.

- The analysis does nothing to increase visibility at a lower *level of detail*. Values are computed by aggregating detailed information into overall project cost risk information.

- The overall *utility* of this type of analysis for actually identifying risk, controlling risk, or planning risk responses is limited. However, this type of analysis can be used to display cost risks known to exist at the cost account level in an aggregate manner (the way some management executives will want to see it).

Summary

This type of analysis model aggregates the cost uncertainty due to risk for any number of cost elements into a distribution of the cost uncertainty for the entire project. It provides the project manager with the information necessary to answer the question: "What is the probability that the project will be complete for X dollars or less?" The distribution also provides the answer to that question's inverse, which is: "How much budget should we assign to this project, based on the risks?" Although various commercial software programs are available to perform this type of analysis, users should be forewarned that the tools provide an aura of certainty to the information they generate. Data developed through a cost risk/WBS simulation model looks extremely accurate and detailed.

Chapter 13

RISK FACTORS

This method is simple to apply. However, getting sound and dependable risk input values for each WBS element can be a challenge. Often the input values are quick judgments made by project personnel. The method does not include procedures for systematic and scientific development of the needed input data. The primary use of the method is to estimate the total added project costs that might be expected due to risks associated with the various project WBS elements.

Technique Description

The basic concept of the risk factor method is to determine factors, or multipliers, with which to increase cost estimates of individual baseline WBS elements to cover anticipated risk-associated cost growth. A reasonable budget above that resulting from the baseline cost estimate is the objective. The method uses a WBS based on a technical breakdown like that shown in Figure 19.

First, the baseline estimate must be developed for each cost element. Applying whatever considerations are appropriate, a risk factor is established for each cost element. This factor generally will be a value between 1.0 (indicating no risk), and 2.0 (indicating so much risk that expected costs would be twice the baseline cost estimate values). Each baseline estimate is then multiplied by its corresponding risk factor to obtain new WBS element cost estimates. These new estimates are summed to derive a budget that will account for technical or other risks.

Obtaining sound WBS element risk factors is the critical aspect of this method and may be difficult. Data analysts have scant documentation to use in substantiating such factors. Because these factors significantly affect analysis results, the input must be obtained from highly experienced technical experts. In other words, the apparent

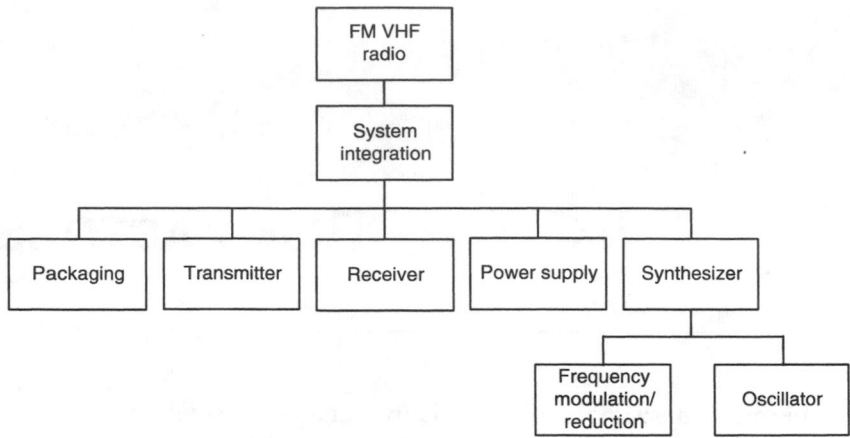

Figure 19. Sample Technical Breakdown

simplicity of the method has not relaxed the requirement that the most experienced project personnel take key roles in the analysis. After a baseline cost estimate is prepared using cost estimating methods, an analyst should be able to prepare a new cost estimate using risk factors expeditiously. The effort will depend on the difficulty an analyst has in obtaining the assistance of technical experts and on how detailed the WBS or cost breakdown is.

When Applicable

Of 57 project management offices responding to a survey on past and current risk analysis utilization, only six had used this technique. Personnel in these six offices found the technique useful primarily for developing project requirements documentation and for project planning. The technique is more applicable early in the life of a project, when information is not available to apply some of the more sophisticated risk analysis techniques. This technique is applicable only when a point-cost estimate, broken out by WBS element, is available. The method's simplicity makes it applicable to even small, low-cost projects.

Input and Output

One primary input of a risk factor assessment is a baseline cost estimate broken out by WBS element. The second primary input is a set of risk factors for each WBS cost element. These factors usually will be subjective judgments of experienced personnel who know the project, its current status, and potential problem areas. The use of checklists or watchlists and the number of items on the lists that apply to each WBS element is one way of helping to judge the level of risk associated with each element.

The output of a risk factor application is a budget or cost estimate that is increased over the baseline budget (or estimate) by an amount required to cover risk-induced costs.

Major Steps in Applying the Technique

The major steps in applying the technique are as follows:

- Obtain a project cost estimate broken out by WBS element. Such estimates should be available; their preparation is not considered to be part of applying this method.

- For each WBS element, obtain an estimate for additional costs (expressed as a percentage of the original estimate) that should be added to accommodate additional work resulting from risks. The opinions of knowledgeable technical and experienced project management personnel should be sought. Reviewing lessons learned for similar systems could also provide insight into how much risk might be involved. If similar tasks have been performed before, and by the same people assigned to the current project, risks should be lower. It is important to remember that past projects were also risky, and therefore, any parametric cost estimates based thereon also include some costs to cover risk.

- Recalculate the total project costs by summing all the WBS element costs, each of which has been adjusted by the corresponding percentage increase to accommodate risks associated with it.

Use of Results

According to the survey of project offices, the risk factor results were found helpful by those offices using them, particularly in the early development of cost estimates during requirements development.

Resource Requirements

Resource requirements for this method can vary greatly. Frequently, the same cost estimator responsible for preparing the baseline cost estimate can also develop the risk factor–adjusted estimates quickly if the appropriate experts provide the WBS element factors in a timely manner. However, applying the method can become more involved as more technical and other experts are used to derive the individual WBS element risk factors.

Reliability

The reliability of this technique can vary widely, both in fact and in the opinion of those reviewing results. Because use of the technique generally requires judgments based on limited information, the knowledge and skill of those making judgments will greatly affect the reliability of the results. Reliability is increased by providing documented justification for all factor values used. A single cost analyst assigning risk level factors for all WBS elements without input from technical and other experts would likely produce relatively low-reliability results.

Selection Criteria

As with each of the chapters on techniques, the risk factors technique is reviewed against selection criteria relating to resource requirements, applications, and output for the technique. To compare risk factors with other techniques, review Table 4.

Resource Requirements

- The *cost* of the technique is generally driven by the time required to develop activity-by-activity breakdowns of the cost estimates, coupled with the time consumed in obtaining WBS activity risk factors from qualified experts.

- The *proper facilities and equipment* for the technique consist of a personal computer loaded with project management and spreadsheet software applications.

- The *time needed to implement* the technique is, much like cost, driven by the resource time consumed in gathering data and assessing risk factors from the experts.

- After the data are developed, the technique has relatively high *ease of use*. The project manager must review the computations and apply them.

- The *project manager's time commitment* normally consists of tracking down the correct experts to provide risk factors for each activity.

Applications

The method applies to product and service projects of virtually any size but can be used only when a cost estimate broken out by WBS element is already available. It can quickly provide a systematically derived estimate of required funds to cover risk-related project costs. The method is best applied when project personnel with experience on other projects are available to provide judgments of the level of risk involved with each WBS element.

- *Project status reporting* is a reasonable use for this approach, because it provides an estimate of the total funds required to complete the project. That figure, coupled with actuals to date, provides the project manager with the baseline status, current status, and potential status of the project at completion.

- *Major planning decisions* may also be driven by the results of the analysis of the technique as described in the previous paragraph.

- *Contract strategy selection* and *milestone preparation* are not typically applications for this technique.

- *Design guidance* can only be supported by this technique from the perspective of the cost implications of different design recommendations.

- *Source selection* is not a prime application for risk factors, because this technique requires a fully developed, comprehensive WBS. Normally at this preliminary stage, such information is not readily available.

- *Budget submittal* can be supported by the technique only if the budget is being developed comprehensively from the bottom up in the WBS. If the exhaustive WBS is not developed for the budget, then the technique will not apply.

Output

- The *accuracy* of this technique is a direct function of the expertise of the experts providing the data for input. This model is the classic example of a "garbage-in, garbage-out" scenario. If the information provided is less than sound, the output will have a low accuracy level. If the experts have extensive experience on similar efforts, the accuracy of the method increases significantly.

- The *level of detail* is low for risk factors, because the technique focuses on a project-wide, rather than a task-by-task, perspective.

- The *utility* of the technique is high as long as the correct goals are sought. If the project manager is looking for project-wide information and a perspective on the overall costs associated with remaining risks, the technique is ideal. For other goals, it would be somewhat inappropriate.

Summary

This analysis method has been used widely to develop an estimate of the funds required to cover added costs resulting from the individual risks associated with specific WBS elements. It is not designed to analyze potential task-by-task overruns, but rather the aggregate overruns for the project.

Chapter 14

PERFORMANCE TRACKING

A U.S. government report on technical risk spent a great deal of time discussing the importance of managing the technical aspects of a project. However, measuring technical risk on any effort that involves furthering the state of the art is difficult and can involve significant risk itself. Performance tracking is conducted by establishing exacting performance criteria for all aspects of the project and assessing them against the acceptable ranges around those criteria. Some concrete measurements are available that can be useful in measuring technical advancement progress against preset goals of projects.

Technique Description

The performance tracking technique advocates using a technical risk assessment report, which is updated periodically. The report is based on working-level data but is intended to provide an overview of current trends and status. The technique uses a set of standard technical indicators proven to be effective measures of technical performance. In addition to the standard measures, the analyst also develops project-unique technical indicators. Each indicator has clearly defined performance projections and preset alert criteria. Standard indicators are shown in Table 7; a sample indicator is shown in Figure 20.

When Applicable

This technique is most effective when objective and quantifiable criteria are established. The technique is best used to manage near-term requirements, but it can be used with minor modifications on any type of project and can be used in conjunction with more elaborate probability-driven risk models to examine corresponding cost-and-schedule effects of current technical performance.

Table 7. Standard Indicators

Technical Risk Indicator (typical unit of measure)	System	Subsystem A	Subsystem B	Subsystem C	Subsystem D	Subsystem E	Statement of work	Contract specifications	Contractor plans	Previous experience
			Applies To						Source	
Design										
Wait time (seconds)	x	x	x	x	x	x		x		
Size	x	x	x	x	x	x		x		
Database access	x	x	x	x	x	x		x		
Throughput	x							x		
Memory utilization (percentage of capacity)	x							x	x	
Design-to-cost (dollars)	x	x	x	x	x	x	x			
Design maturity (number of design deficiencies)	x	x	x	x	x	x	x		x	x
Failure activity (number of failure reports submitted)	x	x	x	x	x	x	x		x	x
Engineering changes (number of engineering change orders)	x	x	x	x	x				x	x
Drawing releases (number of drawings)	x	x	x	x	x				x	x
Engineering resource-hours	x	x	x	x	x				x	x
Test										
Critical test network (scheduled dates for critical test events)	x	x	x	x	x				x	x
Reliability growth (mean time between failures)	x	x	x	x	x			x	x	x
Production										
Transition plan (scheduled dates for critical production events)	x	x	x	x	x				x	x
Delinquent requisitions (number of delinquencies)	x	x	x	x	x				x	x
Production cost (dollars)	x	x	x	x	x		x			
Labor and material requirements (resource-hours unit and material-cost unit)	x	x	x	x	x				x	
Cost										
Cost and schedule performance index (ratio of budgeted and actual costs)	x	x	x	x	x		x			
Estimate at completion (dollars)	x	x	x	x	x				x	
Contingency reserve funds (percentage remaining)	x	x	x	x	x				x	
Management										
Specification verification (number of specification items)	x	x	x	x	x			x		
Major project risk (ranked listing)	x	x	x	x	x					x

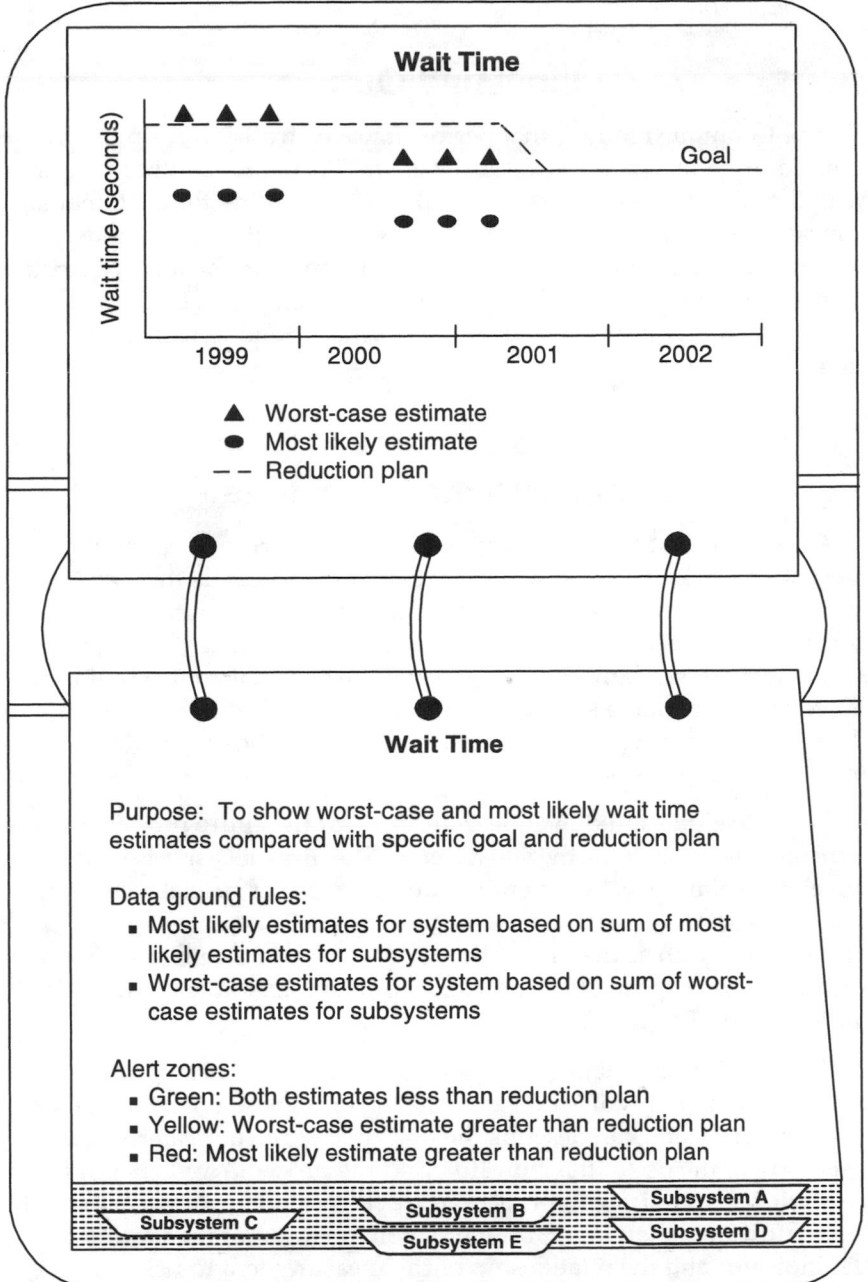

Figure 20. Sample Indicators

Input and Output

The technique requires that performance be tracked on a periodic basis for each technical indicator selected. This requires full cooperation with the various stakeholders in the project, including the customer and any subcontractors. It also requires that subcontractors participate in managing risk (a good benefit). The output can be in the form of a risk management report or a briefing. The contents should include an analysis of each indicator's current performance and longer-term trends.

Major Steps in Applying the Technique

One of the first steps in adapting the technical risk assessment method to track risk performance is to choose indicators that can be applied to the development project. If the project were aircraft construction, weight and size would always be significant. Weight and size may not be as significant on a system to be installed in a building, however. Many of the standard indicators (Table 7) can be used on development projects, and the utility of certain indicators will vary as the project progresses.

The selection should include indicators for the entire project and indicators especially for the subsystems. The unusual aspects of a developmental project frequently require the use of special technical indicators. In the case of space systems, certain indicators are appropriate, such as the production of gasses from the material in the product when exposed to a space environment. Examples of special indicators are listed in Table 8.

Each indicator, whether standard or special, must have ground rules established for data collection and assessment. These can be in the form of a dictionary and can describe the objective of the indicator, why it was chosen, the use of the indicator, and the procedure when a signal is generated that indicates a problem is developing. The dictionary should have sufficient detail to inform the system operator of the meaning of the indicator and the relationship of the measurement to risk.

It is advisable to explain the trends that might be expected during the life of the indicator. Expected values may take many different forms or curve functions but should have traceability to the project goals (cost, schedule, performance, or various combinations). Evaluation criteria

Table 8. Sample Special Indicators

Derived from Specification Requirements	Derived from Program Requirements
■ Performance characteristics: Speed, capacity, accuracy	■ Schedule: Feasibility and probability of timely accomplishment
■ Physical characteristics: Memory utilization, support requirements	■ Resources: Adequacy, distribution
■ Effectiveness characteristics: Reliability, safety, logistics support	■ Test plan: Sufficiency of planned testing
■ Environmental conditions: Platform, workstations	■ Procurement factors: Availability of multiple sources
■ Design and construction: Technology, packaging, materials	

must be set so that they will flag situations that signal problems. Color coding (such as red, yellow, and green for high, medium, and low risk) can be used as can percentage bands for the same type of message. These bands may vary as time progresses: that is, getting tighter as completion is nearing or getting more tolerant as time passes to indicate that a risk is disappearing. In any case, the project manager and any contractors should agree and understand the evaluation criteria chosen and their significance in order to facilitate rapid corrective action.

All this planning would be useless without a formal reporting system. This will vary in form from organization to organization and from manager to manager. It may be produced in report form for presentations to customers and management or stored as raw numerical data points. In any case, it must be in a form that can be immediately used by both contractor and project manager in making critical project decisions. As in any system that requires the coordinated efforts of a matrix organization, someone must ensure that the job is done accurately and in a timely fashion and that proper decision makers are informed of risk situations.

In summary, the major steps in applying risk measurement techniques are as follows:

- ■ Select standard indicators
- ■ Select special indicators
- ■ Establish data definitions
- ■ Project expected trends

- Set the evaluation criteria
- Plan the reporting system
- Assign responsibilities
- Ensure that the job is done accurately and meets deadlines

Use of Results

Technical risk assessment reports furnish information needed to start any action to correct potential problems. Each indicator should be examined separately and then in related groups of indicators. In using the results, analysts must simultaneously consider the factors of cost, schedule, and technical risks.

Resource Requirements

This technique requires personnel with knowledge and skills in highly specialized technical areas. The data received emanate from many functional groups and must be analyzed by people who have skills within the various functional areas. This does not mean that each functional risk assessment area requires a full-time person. It does mean, however, that each functional area may have to contribute expertise.

Reliability

To have a reliable technical risk assessment, all major participants must understand the importance of the assessment and be actively involved in establishing and implementing the system. Each team member should participate in the initial assessment of the project's technical risk and help select indicators to be used in tracking the risk. These same people should provide updates for each reporting period. Raising problems early allows the manager to take action, precluding failure or at least tempering risk.

Supplemental Information

Performance tracking is not new. It has existed in one form or another for many years but has recently surged in popularity and use. Many variations on the theme are presented in this discussion. Control is one of the most critical elements in risk management, and performance tracking is one of the most effective control techniques. Another variation of the method is fully integrated performance measurement.

This is a capability being developed to integrate technical, schedule, and cost performance. It also provides earned value performance measurement capability to project managers who are not getting formal performance data from their contractors or team. The major steps are described in the following sections.

Technical Performance

- Identify specific technical parameters (based on the project's objectives, plans, and specifications) and their value for performance, producibility, quality assurance, reliability, maintainability, supportability, and so on. A few examples (for an aircraft) are shown in Table 9.

- Relate each technical parameter to specific WBS elements whenever practical. Many will relate only to the total system level, but many will come from the specifications, which should match the WBS. In Table 9 for example, the topic of square footage under producibility could be aligned with either an existing WBS activity (such as "Lease construction hangar") or under a separate analysis activity designed exclusively for performance tracking (such as "Evaluate hangar size"). A typical parameter might be "Hangar size is not to exceed 45,000 square feet."

- Define specific methods for calculating, measuring, or observing the value of each technical parameter. For example, it is important to clarify the parameters of how calculations will be derived: "Hangar size evaluations shall include all building square footage used in the actual construction of the aircraft, including all storage areas and housing facilities that are adjacent to the facility."

- Assign a specific individual or organization the responsibility for managing each technical parameter and the progress toward achieving the goal value. In the example of the hangar, a single team member from the maintenance team might be assigned ongoing responsibility to account for any space utilization modifications that occur as the project progresses.

Schedule Performance

- Identify or create specific schedule events at which the calculation or observation is to be made.

Table 9. Fully Integrated Performance Measurement—Typical Technical Parameters

Performance	Producibility
<ul><li>Speed (kn)</li><li>Weight (lb)</li><li>Range (NM)</li><li>Power (kW)</li><li>Turn rate (deg/sec)</li><li>Takeoff distance (ft)</li><li>Climb rate (ft/sec)</li><li>Accuracy (ft)</li><li>Radar cross section (sq ft)</li></ul>	<ul><li>Capital ($)</li><li>Human resources (number of people)</li><li>Facilities (sq ft)</li><li>Material ($)</li><li>Equipment (machinery required)</li><li>Schedule (time)</li><li>Risk (1.0–2.0)</li></ul>

Quality Assurance	Reliability
<ul><li>Scrap, rework, and repair (% of labor)</li><li>Yield (% of first-time inspection successes)</li><li>Supplier rating (%)</li><li>Quality costs ($)</li><li>Customer satisfaction (0–1.0)</li><li>Software lines of code (LOC) in violation per 1,000 LOC</li></ul>	<ul><li>Mean time between failures (MTBF) (hr/days)</li><li>Mean time to repair (MTTR) (hr/days)</li><li>Probability of component/assembly failure (0–1.0)</li><li>Life-cycle analysis ($)</li><li>Design-to-cost ($)</li></ul>

Supportability	Maintainability
<ul><li>Parts inventory ($)</li><li>Costs ($)</li><li>Resources (human, equipment, facilities)</li><li>Modularity (%)</li><li>Operational availability (%)</li><li>MTBF (hr/days)</li><li>MTTR (hr/days)</li></ul>	<ul><li>Standardization (%)</li><li>Modularity (%)</li><li>Update ability (0–1.0)</li><li>Special equipment ($)</li><li>Frequency (how often, how long)</li><li>Costs ($)</li></ul>

- Determine values or conditions to be achieved at each milestone. Also set a tolerance or alarm value to represent a threshold for corrective action.

- Identify or create a specific schedule event at which the goal is to be achieved.

- Identify whether calculation or observation will be used to assess the event at various points in time.

A plot of the technical performance parameter value against time gives a visual portrayal of the relationship between technical performance and schedule (see Figure 21 and Table 10).

Cost Performance

- Assign budgets to each technical performance parameter. These budgets may be real and add up to contractual values, or they may be fictitious units created just to determine relative weights. These budgets can be assigned in many different ways—the only requirements are rationality, traceability, and consistency.

- Distribute the assigned budgets to each of the measurement milestones based on engineering judgment of the percentage of the total value associated with each milestone.

- Use conventional earned value techniques to measure accomplishment (such as 50-50 milestones).

- Apply the schedule performance index to appropriate activities in the resource-loaded network to determine the cost impact of the technical and schedule performance.

A quick example may help clarify the technique. As shown in Table 10, performance parameter 1 has a numeric goal. A method of calculating progress against the goal has been derived. At selected milestone 1, progress against the goal is calculated (CALC). By selected milestone 3, progress against the goal can be observed (OBS); by milestone 5, the goal should be attained (GOAL).

Selection Criteria

As with each of the chapters on techniques, performance tracking is reviewed against selection criteria relating to resource requirements, applications, and output for the technique. To compare performance tracking with other techniques, review Table 4.

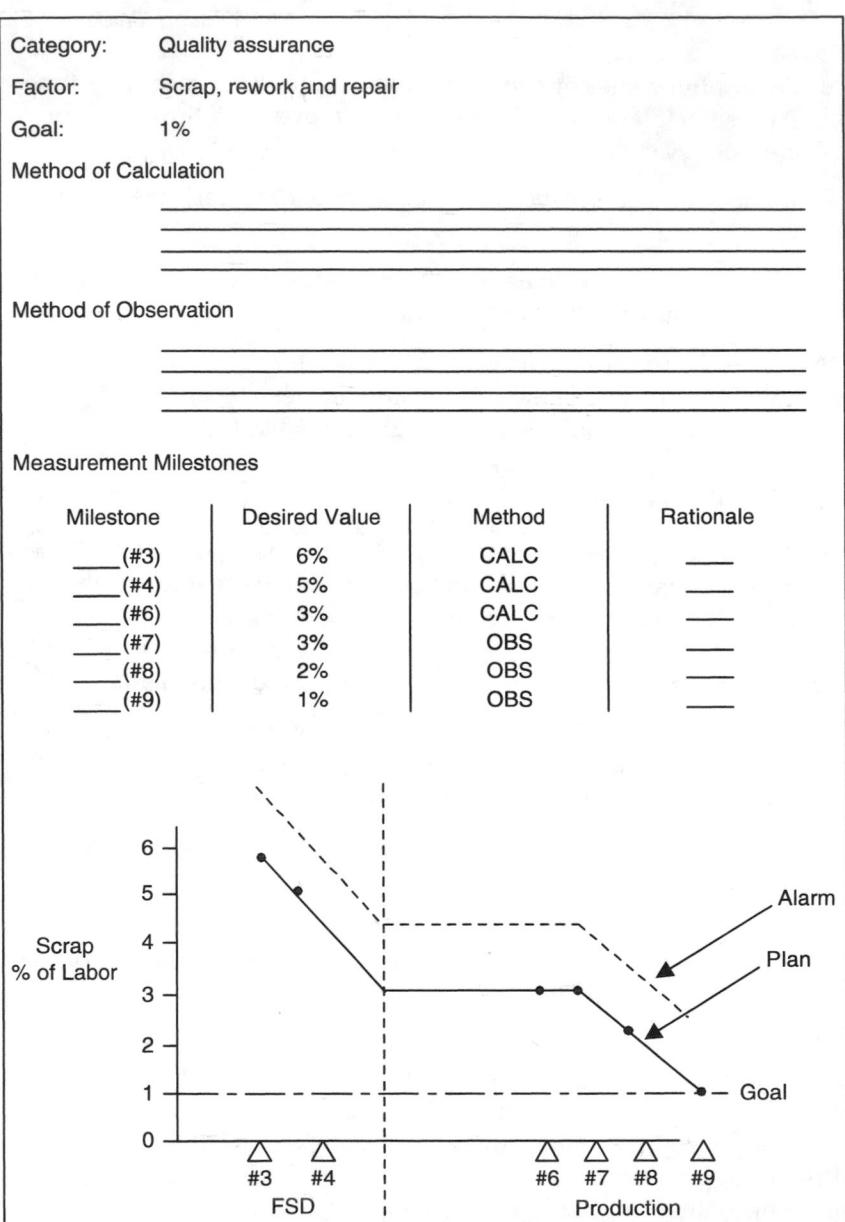

Category: Quality assurance

Factor: Scrap, rework and repair

Goal: 1%

Method of Calculation

Method of Observation

Measurement Milestones

Milestone	Desired Value	Method	Rationale
____ (#3)	6%	CALC	____
____ (#4)	5%	CALC	____
____ (#6)	3%	CALC	____
____ (#7)	3%	OBS	____
____ (#8)	2%	OBS	____
____ (#9)	1%	OBS	____

Figure 21. Technical Performance Management

Table 10. Technical Performance Schedule Milestones

Parameter	Spec or Goal	Development Project Specific Milestones					Production Project Specific Milestones					Ops
		1	2	3	4	5	6	7	8	9	10	Ops
Performance												
Parameter 1	V_{GOAL}	V_{CALC}		V_{OBS}	V_{OBS}	V_{GOAL}						
Parameter 2	V_{GOAL}		V_{CALC}	V_{OBS}	V_{GOAL}							
Parameter 3	V_{GOAL}			V_{CALC}		V_{OBS}		V_{OBS}	V_{GOAL}			
•												
•												
Quality Assurance												
SCRAP	1_{GOAL}			6_{CALC}	5_{CALC}		3_{CALC}	3_{OBS}	2_{OBS}	1_{OBS}		
Factor 2	V_{GOAL}					V_{CALC}		V_{OBS}			V_{GOAL}	
Factor 3	V_{GOAL}	V_{CALC}		V_{CALC}			V_{OBS}	V_{GOAL}				
•												
•												
Reliability												
Parameter 1	V_{GOAL}	V_{CALC}	V_{CALC}	V_{CALC}	V_{OBS}	V_{OBS}	V_{OBS}	V_{GOAL}				
Parameter 2	V_{GOAL}											
•												
•												
Maintainability												
Condition 1	C_{GOAL}		C_1		C_2			C_3	C_{GOAL}			
Condition 2	C_{GOAL}	C_1	C_2			C_3			C_{GOAL}			
•												
•												
Supportability												
Condition 1	C_{GOAL}			C_1		C_2			C_3			C_{GOAL}
•												
•												
Producibility												
Parameter 1	V_{GOAL}	V_{CALC}		V_{OBS}	V_{OBS}		V_{GOAL}					
Parameter 2	V_{GOAL}		V_{CALC}	V_{OBS}		V_{GOAL}						

Resource Requirements

- The *cost* of the performance tracking technique is limited if the systems are already in place and it is maintained on an ongoing basis. Setting up the initial indicators is somewhat time consuming and should be done with excruciating care.

- The *proper facilities and equipment* are also limited, because little more than a spreadsheet is required to track the data and maintain accurate project records.

- If the entire team and the project manager commit to performance tracking from the beginning of the project, their *time needed to implement* will be minimal on an individual basis. Collectively, however, the time appears more significant. If the project manager decides to implement performance tracking at midproject, significant initiative with extensive time commitments will be required.

- The *ease of use* of the technique is a function of the clarity of instruction provided by the project manager for the effort. Although performance tracking is not overly complex, it does require clear direction for the uninitiated.

- The *project manager's time commitment* for the effort primarily stems from ensuring total involvement in the process, including all team members and contractors.

Applications

This technique can be used in most of the categories in Table 4. Because the technique focuses on monitoring progress after an item is assigned, using it in the resource allocation process is of little value.

- *Project status reporting* is a key asset of this technique. Although there are schedule tracking tools (like earned value) and cost tracking tools (like budgets and interim reports), performance tracking affords the project manager a means to quantify and report on quality and requirements achieved. No other tools go to quite this level of depth in establishing specific values for the activities as they relate to requirements.

- *Major planning decisions* can be driven by the results of performance tracking, because the information derived from the technique points to areas of organizational expertise and weakness. Most organizations strive to find projects and approaches that take advantage of their strengths. Performance tracking is an excellent technique for identifying what those strengths may be.

- *Contract strategy selection* is both support for and supported by performance tracking. The strategy to support performance tracking will incorporate detailed reporting (to mirror the systems deployed by the host organization) by the vendor or subcontractor. Performance tracking supports contract strategy selection by building, over time, a historic database that includes information on how the organization has performed against specific types of activities and, therefore, in relation to specific types of subcontractors and vendors.

- In *milestone preparation,* performance tracking allows for a completely different type of milestone. Rather than identifying milestones for a percentage of schedule achieved or a percentage of costs spent, performance tracking allows for milestones developed against degrees of anticipated customer satisfaction achieved, based on performance to date. It can be used to establish triggers and thresholds for risk, which can then be converted into project milestones.

- *Design guidance* is supported in much the same fashion as major planning decisions. Performance tracking identifies strengths, allowing the project manager to endorse designs that work with the organization's high-skill areas.

- *Source selection* may be driven by performance tracking, particularly if there is an established database of performance tracking numbers. Performance tracking identifies responsibility for tasks that are at the designated level of quality and for tasks that are not high quality. That affords the project manager a quantitative measure to apply in assessing past performance of vendors.

- *Budget submittal* is supported by performance tracking primarily as an element of the budget's cost. Project managers need to account for the costs associated with performance tracking. But the development of performance tracking data also gives the project manager a much more detailed analysis of each of the work packages and what it will take to achieve quality with them. As such, a budget submitted after an initial performance tracking review may be far more accurate than one developed without using the technique.

Output

The output of the technique is very good in general. If appropriate indicators are selected, a quantified measure for each potential problem area is graphically presented. This information is extremely useful for project management as well as management communication.

- The *accuracy* of the technique is driven primarily by the indicators selected, the measures used to assess those indicators, and the personnel responsible for tracking the performance in the context of those indicators.

- Most project managers would consider the *level of detail* associated with performance tracking to be extensive. Because the technique requires a thoughtful, painstaking review of each work package to determine its contributions to a quality output, the level of detail is often much finer than is normally developed in a project without performance tracking.

- The main *utility* of the technique is in tracking project quality and providing management communication both internally and to the customer. By tracking all the various aspects of the project and the deliverables, the project manager can, on short notice, develop comprehensive analyses of the organization's ability to provide the deliverables as promised to the customer.

Summary

The performance tracking technique challenges the project team to meet preordained success criteria for each element of the project. No single significant component is overlooked, and team members clearly understand what is expected of them. In many organizations, that is a significant shift from an attitude that pushes team members toward a satisfactory overall deliverable to the customer. Performance tracking propels the organization toward higher levels of quality.

Chapter 15

OTHER COMMON
TECHNIQUES

Cost Performance
Reports Analysis

Cost performance reports (CPRs) have become useful in uncovering areas in which technical problems are causing variances. In these reports, team members explain cost and schedule variances using narrative to indicate the specific problem causing the variance. Many of the variances reported can signal risk situations as they are developing, such as late vendor or subcontractor deliveries. Continuing these types of schedule slips can put an entire project schedule at risk. Normally, project managers are limited in what they can do to alleviate these situations, except when the sponsoring organization is causing the delays. In such cases, problems sometimes can be alleviated by high-level coordination with the sponsoring organization. However, this does not always work. For example, tight control over a highly specialized, highly technical subcontractor may not be very effective and the risk of inaccurate specialty work may give rise to risks in other areas of the project.

Just as risk may be driven by cost variance, cost variances can also be driven by risk. Cost growth must be considered a significant risk item. The CPR is designed to display cost growth as a variance and then to discuss that variance in terms of cause, effect, and corrective actions that might alleviate the situation.

If the project is using the CPR as a cost reporting tool, it also should be used for risk assessment and analysis. The discussion of variances in that report can contain data vital to risk identification, quantification, and response development. The report may also present new and previously undiscovered risks. These risks should then be investigated to ascertain their effects on the project.

Independent Technical Assessment

An independent technical assessment is nothing more than a formal technical review conducted by an expert (or experts) in the field to determine the potential of the project for achieving specific objectives. An independent technical assessment requires personnel other than those subordinate to the project manager and, therefore, will always require approval by some higher level of authority. The timing of such reviews is critical. If problems are found, there must be time to correct them before any critical milestone reviews. This technique has been cited for substantially reducing project risk, especially that associated with multi-organizational involvement.

Technique Description

A team of experts from outside the project office reviews a number of specified aspects of the project. The team usually consists of senior personnel who can make timely evaluations of project activities and progress based on their extensive experience. Team size can vary with the size of the project and the number of issues the team is chartered to review. The entire process is usually limited to 4 to 8 weeks of near-full-time effort. The final product is almost always a briefing to the sponsor or manager authorizing the review as well as a written report.

When Applicable

This technique can be used to support design reviews. It can also be used to address perceptions of a troubled project. A good time for an independent technical assessment is when a project is (or is perceived to be) in trouble. If the trouble is real, this technique will give the project manager added credibility and will quiet critics. When possible, such reviews should be scheduled to cause minimum disruption of milestone activities. An independent technical assessment is usually more appropriate during system development than during actual implementation or production.

Input and Output

The input will vary widely depending on the issues to be addressed and the team members' expertise. Team members will obtain the information they need through briefings by the project team, reviews of project documentation, interviews, and visits to project facilities. The expertise and experience team members bring with them is an important input. The most common output is a briefing to the sponsor or manager. Other stakeholders may be brought into the briefing, as appropriate. The briefing must address each of several criteria or issues defined at the outset of the review. It also should include recommendations for follow-up action.

Major Steps in Applying the Technique

The following procedure is common to most independent technical assessments:

- Upper management (with control over the expert resources required) calls for the review.

- The project manager and upper management specify issues to be addressed.

- The project manager and upper management form the review team.

- The team gathers the required information about project objectives, status, resources, and activities.

- The team analyzes the information gathered.

- The team and the project manager present their results to the authority requesting the review and to other appropriate stakeholders.

Use of Results

Independent technical assessments are useful for design, contracting strategy, planning, and implementation coordination. When review results are favorable, project risk is reduced immediately. An associated benefit is the ability to meet pending milestone reviews.

Resource Requirements

Two types of resources are required to carry out an independent technical assessment. First, as many as 10 experts may be needed to form the review team. (Team size will depend largely on the expertise required and the magnitude of the project.) The team should include experienced personnel from the middle management level or higher. These people should anticipate having to commit roughly half their time for the duration of the effort.

In addition to team resource requirements, the project manager must arrange a number of informational briefings and interviews to provide the review team with the required information quickly. If review team members are from off-site locations, the project manager may have substantial administrative tasks in dealing with the needs of out-of-town guests.

Reliability

The reliability of an independent technical assessment is usually high. The reliability depends somewhat on the quality of team members—their recognized level of expertise. Although team independence is essential, cooperation between the team and the project manager is also essential. The project manager must provide all required information, and the review team must present a balanced picture, rather than focusing on the most negative areas. The major disadvantage of an independent technical assessment is that it can disrupt other project activities. This is especially true if it uncovers deficiencies and there is not enough time for corrective actions before an important milestone. Therefore, the reviewed schedule is an important consideration.

Selection Criteria

The selection criteria for this technique are all rather positive. Independent technical assessments do not place great demands on any single resource during the project, although there is some time required by the project manager to support the individual or team. Many organizations require project managers to submit periodic jeopardy reports, which mirror much of the information generated by independent technical assessments. The technique has applications across the life cycle of the project and provides other key pieces of data that can readily be incorporated into the historic project database every organization should maintain. The output, since it reflects an individual or group perspective, may be marginally less accurate than other techniques, but the level of detail and utility of the technique is without peer. It is easy to understand, requires little training, and provides valuable real-time information.

Independent Cost Estimates

Independent cost estimates must be developed one or more times for many projects, depending on the level of control demanded by the sponsoring organization. Historically, these estimates have been driven by the perception that project managers, because of their commitment to achieving project goals, naturally tend to be optimistic regarding the risks and costs of the project, particularly in the early stages. To provide decision makers with data reflecting an independent viewpoint, independent cost estimates became popular. The concept was that cost estimators, being outside the influence of the project, would develop estimates that more accurately portray the challenges, risks, and costs associated with developing and implementing projects.

An independent cost estimate basically entails the same procedures, methodologies, and techniques that would be used to accomplish any major project cost estimate. Ideally, the independent estimate should select methodologies and techniques different from those that underlie the original cost estimate. In addition, the independent cost estimate should incorporate a detailed comparison of the two approaches and explain the differences.

The key aspect of the independent cost estimate is that it is developed in organizational channels separate from the project. This helps it serve as an analytical tool to validate or cross-check estimates developed by the project manager. This second opinion helps avoid the risk that some significant costs have been overlooked or that the project manager's sense of advocacy has resulted in low estimates that could jeopardize the success of the project.

To the extent that those preparing independent cost estimates are advised and supported by a technical staff independent of the project team, some independent assessment of technical risks may also be accomplished while preparing the cost estimate.

The selection criterion for independent cost estimates is that it is resource intensive and thus may not be approved by management for all but the most significant projects. The applications for the technique are almost exclusive to the beginning of the project or major design decision points. The output from the technique varies widely in value, because the organization may or may not be equipped to handle the information this technique provides.

Chapter 16

RISK RESPONSE CONTROL

Although the concepts and techniques of risk planning, identification, quantification, and response development are complex, the greater challenge is in implementing the risk management process. Project managers are almost categorically overcommitted and overextended. In a risk analysis and management survey, allocating resources to implement an effective risk management program was a significant and frequently reported problem. More than 50 percent of the project managers responded that inadequate project staffing was a major risk.

Risk response control as an additional requirement for the project team can seem overwhelming. But risk management is an integral part of project management, not an additional task. Risk management affects each classic element of management (planning, organizing, directing, and controlling) and plays an important role in decision making. In essence, risk management is a subset of sound project management. And although the level of activity may vary, risk management should be viewed as an ongoing process, rather than a one-time exercise.

Risk response control is incorporating risk management concepts and techniques into the project management process, not simply manipulating a certain model. To this end, this chapter provides guidance for organizing for risk management, communicating risk data, and developing a risk management capability.

Organizing for Risk Management

The project manager establishes the goals for the risk management effort, allocates the resources to accomplish these objectives, and oversees the process. However, risk management is a significant responsibility in each functional manager's job. Risk is typically discovered in the functional analysis and decision-making process. Figure 22 depicts a sample functional analysis that involves the complex interplay of technical, programmatic, supportability, cost, and schedule risk. Functional managers must understand the implications risk has in their respective disciplines. The project manager, who ultimately is responsible for implementing risk management, provides the motivation and structure to manage risk effectively and promotes continual interaction and communication between team members.

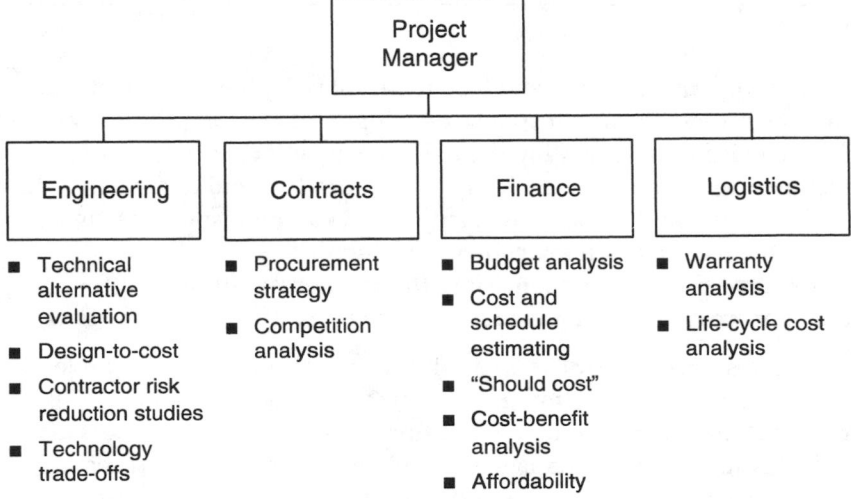

Figure 22. Functional Roles in Risk Management

The greatest variable in implementing a risk management process is team organization. A survey of risk management activities in the project management offices revealed two approaches that the respondents felt were successful. One group of project managers designated specific positions to conduct the project's risk management efforts. The number of people allocated varied by the size of the project and the techniques used. Other project managers felt that risk management was such an integral part of project management that they did not designate separate personnel to manage risk. They felt that risk was adequately considered in the normal performance of their jobs. Either approach is defensible.

Three basic themes stand out as guidelines for incorporating risk management into the project management process:

- The project manager is ultimately responsible.

- Risk management is a team function.

- Risk management activities and responsibilities assigned to groups are, in effect, not assigned; actions should be explicit and assignments clear.

Communicating
Risk Data

An important aspect of risk management implementation (which, if ignored, can make the best risk assessment and analysis ineffective and incomplete) is properly communicating risk data to decision makers. Terms must be defined clearly. Information must be presented clearly and consistently. Risk data must be thoroughly documented if risk management is to be effective.

No standards exist for defining terms for risk. Although this book presents a basic framework for discussing risk, an argument can be made that no universal standard *can* be used to compare risk across projects. Given these circumstances, the terminology used to present risk-related data must be clear and unambiguous to ensure common understanding among project participants and upper management.

For a full understanding of risk information, the process and content of the risk management effort also must be captured and communicated. Sources of data; assumptions made about the project; the assessment, analysis, and handling techniques used; and the sensitivity to change all must be consistently documented and communicated.

The documentation supporting subjective issues such as "sensitivity to change" will vary based on the project, the project manager, and the business climate. However, it is important that the project manager note (in the project binder) the criteria that will drive the need for reevaluating the risk and the risk selection technique.

Although the subject of risk is complex, presenting findings and risk data should be straightforward and clear. Depicting a cumulative probability distribution function from a Monte Carlo network analysis may be informative to an analyst, but it is meaningless to most decision makers. Risk data must be presented in a usable format that communicates the essential elements of the risk management effort.

Developing a Risk Management Capability

The discussion of risk management implementation typically centers around evaluating and selecting tools and techniques to be used and the source of resources to use them. Much of this chapter has focused on those two topics. Figure 23 shows the four basic elements of risk management that support the implementation of the process. Each element should be considered when developing a risk management capability.

Although resources and technique selection are essential to risk management, training and procedures are also critical for successful implementation. Training in the concepts and techniques is required for full understanding and effective accomplishment of an organization's risk management objectives. Training project personnel is critical to fully reap the benefits of the risk management effort. Whether contained in a formal plan or not, procedures should be developed that establish direction and responsibility for the risk management process.

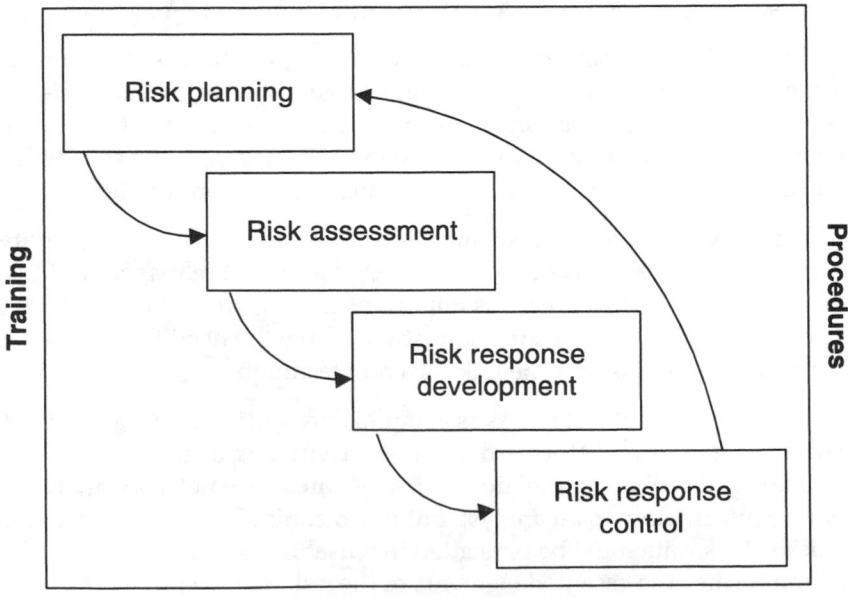

Figure 23. Risk Management Process

CONTRACTOR RISK MANAGEMENT

Organizational Responsibilities

In putting work out to bid, the purchasing agency must accept the fact that risk management is a key part of a procurement strategy. A formal plan of risk assessment and response is best established by the organization very early in each major project or program. This plan considers the contractor risks and internal organizational risks. Assessment and analysis of each significant element of project risk should continue throughout the purchasing or procurement cycle. The procurement strategy ought to be designed to lower risks to acceptable levels. The internal purchasing or contracting agency should include requirements in the requests for proposals (RFPs) for risk management on the part of the contractors. If the process is followed well, contractors will have to stipulate their approach to identifying and managing risks inherent in the project.

Good procurement strategies incorporate demands that the contractors will provide their own risk management plans and risk assessment reports to bolster internal efforts. Similarly, in an ideal world, all RFPs would include a clear request for identifying project risks and trade-offs and an understanding of who bears those risks.

Sample statements that could be used in RFPs follow (DSMC, 1986).

Engineering/Design

The offeror shall describe the engineering/technical tasks to be accomplished during the project that contribute to risk reduction. The discussion shall contain the following item:

A discussion of major technical risk items associated with the offeror's proposed concept, including payoffs that will potentially result from the proposed approach, as well as problem areas. The approach to determining the technical risks involved in your project and your approach to reducing such risks to acceptable levels shall be described. Key development issues and the proposed solution approach shall be identified. The discussion shall present the criteria to be used to evaluate critical decision points and information requirements, and the process to be used to develop, evaluate, and implement fallback positions as required.

Reliability and Maintainability (Quality)

Describe your approach to determining the technical risk involved in your reliability and maintainability (quality) programs and your approach to reducing such risks to acceptable levels. This discussion shall present the criteria you plan to use in determining the criticality of technologies; the techniques used to evaluate critical decision points and information requirements; and the process used to develop, evaluate, and implement fallback positions as required.

Quality in Design

Identify quality in design risks, and factor these risks into design trade-off studies.

Producibility

Describe the approach to determining the technical risk involved with your capacity to produce and the approach to reducing such risks to acceptable levels. This discussion shall present the criteria you plan to use in determining the criticality of technologies; the techniques used to evaluate critical decision points and information requirements; and the process used to develop, evaluate, and implement fallback positions as required.

Manufacturing Research/Technology

Provide an assessment of the likelihood that the design concept can be produced using existing technology while meeting quality, cost, and schedule requirements. Include an evaluation of the capability to follow through on the design concept, including requirements for critical process capabilities and special facilities development. Also include tests and demonstrations required for new materials and alternative approaches, anticipating implementation risks, potential cost and schedule impacts, and surge capabilities.

Project Control System

Describe your risk management approach. Discuss how information from functional areas will be integrated into the risk management process.

Planning

Describe the initial planning accomplished in the following areas: risk identification, risk resolution, risk control implementation, fallback position identification, resource requirements, critical materials, and critical processes. Also identify risks associated with any long lead-time requirements, management systems, organizational requirements, staffing, and scheduling.

Quality Assurance

Describe any quality assurance risks you foresee for this project and the actions planned to reduce those risks.

Evaluation Summary

The overall evaluation of each proposal may include on-site inspections and results of preaward surveys to provide information to the contracting authority. This information may include offeror's current and future capability to perform all aspects of the project. Risk assessment associated with the major areas of the project will be accomplished. In assessing risk, an independent judgment of the probability of success, the impact of failure, and the alternatives available to meet the requirements will be considered.

Contractor Responsibilities

The contractor must be made aware through the language in the contract that the information contained in its response will be used for risk analysis. The contractor should be responsible for making a thorough assessment of risks in its proposal. The contractor should include sufficient information to convince the purchasing authority that the contractor recognizes and has quantified the risk inherent in the project. The proposal should identify areas in which actions by the organization can support risk reduction. These areas can include items such as long lead-time funding and the need for approval of priority status for materials.

In proposing a risk management system, the contractor should highlight how it can use existing internal systems to provide information on risk. The contractor should also focus on how it can include risk management in its normal management practices and in its regular communication with the organization.

AN ABBREVIATED LIST OF RISK SOURCES

An exhaustive list of risk sources would be as long as the dictionary (or longer). The sources listed in Table B-1 represent only a small percentage of the *possible* sources. However, this list of risk sources includes risks that are most common and prevalent in the community that created it. This list was generated for a bureaucratic organization focusing on field deployment of large-scale hardware and software systems and engaged in intense activity on short notice. This may or may not describe your organizational environment. However, this background information should provide some perspective on why these sources were selected above all others.

Risk sources are where the risks originate. Risk sources are not categories, although treating them as categories could help identify and define other risks. Categories sort risks to aid in identification. Sources generate risks.

Table B-1. Possible Risk Sources

Risk	Cost	Project	Schedule	Technical	Comments
Capacity				x	The lack of facilities and tools to produce at the desired rate (rate tooling) could prevent production flow from reaching the desired level.

Table B-1—*Continued*

Risk	Cost	Project	Schedule	Technical	Comments
Concept, failure to apply logistics support analysis (LSA) during concept exploration				x	Failure to participate in the definition of system concepts could produce a system design in follow-on phases that does not meet supportability objectives and requires excessive or unattainable operation and support (O&S) costs, as well as labor, to meet the readiness objectives.
Concurrency	x		x		Concurrent development or preparation for production could cause deviations. Concurrency often results in discovery of problems at a time when a cost premium must be paid to resolve problems and keep the project on or near the original schedule.
Configuration control of vendor products				x	Organizations do not control the configuration of items procured from the marketplace, which presents potential risks in both initial design and availability of spares.
Contracting, inadequate provision for support	x				In terms of impact and the probability of its occurrence, the major risk area in integrated logistics support (ILS) contracting is the failure to contract properly for data, materials, and services.
Contractor, communication by		x			Failure of the subcontractors' and contractors' personnel to keep prime contractor and project management organization informed of problems and potential problems in a timely manner. Communication problems may also occur if management fails to fully communicate direction to all involved in the project in a timely manner.
Contractor, lack of financial strength of	x		x		If any contractors have not been able to adequately finance project requirements, the required work may be delayed or curtailed.

Table B-1—*Continued*

Risk	Cost	Project	Schedule	Technical	Comments
Contractor, production readiness of			x		A contractor may fail to be adequately prepared for production.
Contractor, subcontractors and control of		x			A prime contractor may not maintain adequate control of subcontractor quantity, schedule, and cost performance.
Contractor, underbidding by	x		x		A contractor may underbid or buy in to get contracts and may fail to provide the desired products and services on schedule and within budget.
Coordination, inadequate	x	x			Organizations often fail to coordinate purchases with other departments or divisions, which minimizes available logistics support and the economies of scale that would otherwise be available.
Data, inadequate planning for utilization of				x	Collecting data without detailed planning for its use may lead to a mismatch of data collection information requirements and failure to accomplish the intended purpose of the assessment.
Data, incomplete or inaccessible			x	x	Without sufficient data available from each test and used properly for planning subsequent tests, it is not possible to evaluate the adequacy of the system to meet all readiness requirements. Without accurate failure rates, system and component reliability cannot be determined. Lacking the necessary data, system design and ILS progress cannot be established, problems cannot be identified, and additional testing may be required.
Design, delayed definition of logistics criteria			x		Delayed decisions on reliability and supportability requirements could result in suboptimum support. After the design is committed, the options become limited.

Table B-1—*Continued*

Risk	Cost	Project	Schedule	Technical	Comments
Design, impact of engineering changes	x				A high number of design changes made during development could overwhelm ILS planning and create an inability to reflect ILS and O&S cost considerations fully in engineering change decisions.
Design, invalid application of component reliability and maintainability (R&M) data		x			Design and manufacture determines the mean life and failure rate of components when viewed in isolation. The consequences of improperly computed material replacement rates are invalid labor requirements, incorrect supply support stockage lists, and invalid repair level analyses.
Design, lack of life-cycle cost (LCC) impact on design and logistics support process	x			x	LCC is most effective when it is integrated into the engineering and management process that makes design and logistics engineering choices. This integration must start at project initiation. Failure to implement LCC throughout may result in costly reworking, test failures, contract termination costs, and increased O&S costs.
Design, unrealistic R&M requirements	x		x		Unrealistic R&M requirements could lead to increased design and development costs incurred as a result of excessive design iterations.
Design stability	x		x		There may be lack of design stability during the production phase.
Engineering, late establishment of readiness and supportability objectives	x		x	x	The system engineering process is a key factor in identifying and attaining realistic readiness and supportability objectives. If a well-organized process is not started at the project inception and continued throughout the development phases, then the project risks are increased design, development, and O&S costs; schedule delays; and degraded readiness factors.

Table B-1—*Continued*

Risk	Cost	Project	Schedule	Technical	Comments
Engineering, site survey results		x	x		Historical or archaeological site survey findings could delay site construction and cause significant deployment problems.
Environmental impact	x		x		Natural disasters (such as fires, floods, storms, earthquakes) may occur.
Equipment, common support	x		x		Common support equipment may not be available to operate and maintain the system.
Failure to structure or tailor LSA requirements	x		x	x	Failure to establish an LSA plan specifically designed to meet the needs of the material system could result in excessive costs, the performance of unwanted analysis while failing to complete needed studies, and the development of excessive documentation while overlooking critical information needs.
Familiarization		x			Contractor personnel may be unfamiliar with the systems or equipment or may lack experience producing similar systems or equipment.
Familiarization, tolerance levels		x			Difficulties in achieving closer than usual tolerance levels may occur.
Fault detection				x	A failure to obtain designed performance may be detected.
Funding, advanced buy authorization limitations	x				Long lead-time requirements may create problems if there is insufficient advanced-buy funding to meet the needs of the project.
Funding, constraints on	x				Lack of timely receipt of project funds may cause delays.

Table B-1—*Continued*

Risk	Cost	Project	Schedule	Technical	Comments
Funding, long-term	x		x		The requirement to execute a project over a period of time with funds provided through a fiscal-year-to-fiscal-year agreement may result in constraints.
Inflation	x				Levels of inflation significantly higher than originally forecast may increase costs.
Integration/ interface		x			New and unique requirements (such as adaptability, compatibility, interface standard, and interpretability) may delay the project.
Joint partner project decision			x		Problems and delays resulting from reduced joint partner participation or other user decisions could disrupt the project.
Labor disputes	x		x		Labor difficulties (such as strikes, lockouts, slowdowns) could increase costs and delay schedules.
Legal disputes	x		x		Award and performance disputes and related legal actions could delay a project.
Legislation	x				Higher taxes, new labor laws affecting pay and benefits, social security increases, and so on, could increase costs.
Maintainability				x	Failure to achieve maintainability using a design that is compatible with established maintenance procedures may force changes in the maintenance approach.
Material properties	x				Material property requirements beyond those usually expected may increase costs.
Modeling validity		x			Inaccuracies in models used to develop mathematical and physical predictions may disrupt the project.
Objectives and strategies		x			Changes in objectives and strategies may disrupt the project.

Table B-1—*Continued*

Risk	Cost	Project	Schedule	Technical	Comments
Operating environment				x	Performing in an unusually harsh environment could increase technical difficulties.
Operating policies		x			Changes in operating policies may affect system or system support requirements.
Personnel, available skills of		x			The shortage of personnel with technical, management, and other skills needed to carry out internal and contractor activities may disrupt the project.
Personnel, downsizing and streamlining of	x			x	Initiatives on downsizing and streamlining could impose restrictions on the project manager as well as the designer early in the definition of requirements. Although intended to decrease cost and improve efficiency, casual application of such guidance could result in a loss of standardization, attendant cost increases, and loss of documented lessons-learned experience.
Personnel, forced placement of		x			If the project has several inadequate personnel and managers, either internally or under key contractors, seriously counterproductive events could occur.
Personnel, security clearances of			x		Any delays in obtaining required personnel security clearances could delay the schedule.
Physical properties	x				Different-than-expected dynamics, stress, thermal, or vibration requirements could increase costs.
Planning, delayed facilities			x		Failure to perform timely facility planning could result in substantial deployment delays.

Table B-1—*Continued*

Risk	Cost	Project	Schedule	Technical	Comments
Planning, delayed postproduction support				x	Continued support of the material system by the industrial base existing in the post-production time frame might not be economically feasible.
Planning, updating deployment		x		x	Unreported and uncorrected deployment problems could generate a serious flaw in an updated deployment plan.
Policies, new		x			Added workload or time requirements brought about by new direction or policy may disrupt the project.
Priority			x		Problems resulting from changing the priority assigned to the project and thereby timely access to testing facilities, funds, materials, and so on, could delay the schedule.
Project stretchout			x		Direction to slip the project schedule from the original plan may disrupt the project.
Radiation properties				x	Increased radiation stress resistance requirements could cause technical difficulties.
Reliability	x		x		Failure to forecast system reliability properly may affect predicted reliability growth.
Scarce resources	x		x		Shortages of critical materials, components, or parts may disrupt the project.
Scheduling, accelerated acquisition	x				Lead times for delivery of nondevelopmental items could be extremely short, particularly for in-stock items. This poses a substantial risk of deployment with incomplete or inadequate logistic support and attendant degraded readiness.

Table B-1—*Continued*

Risk	Cost	Project	Schedule	Technical	Comments
Scheduling, accelerated projects	x		x		An accelerated system development project may be required to overcome a critical deficiency in an existing capability. This "streamlining" could pose the risk of delaying design maturation with frequent configuration changes occurring in late development.
Scheduling, accelerated projects	x				Compressed schedules increase the demand for critical assets during the time of normal asset shortages, which could create unrecoverable delays.
Scheduling, decision delay			x		Disruption of the project schedule may result from delays in obtaining higher-level approval to award contracts, proceed to the next phase, and so on.
Scheduling, excessive lead times			x		Lead times for critical components or services that are longer than expected may delay the schedule.
Scheduling, slippage			x		Failure to understand how slippage in one functional element affects other elements and milestone events could ultimately delay the entire project.
Service roles and mission changes	x		x		Problems may cause deviations from the project resulting from changing service roles and missions that significantly alter the planned use of the system.
Software design			x		Unique software test requirements and unsatisfactory software test results could result in changes in the basic project.
Software language			x		A new computer language or one unfamiliar to those responsible for planning and writing software could cause schedule delays.

Table B-1—*Continued*

Risk	Cost	Project	Schedule	Technical	Comments
State-of-the-art advances, lack of supporting		x			Advances from other projects that might not be as expected could significantly affect the current project.
State-of-the-art advances, major		x		x	Problems resulting from greater-than-anticipated advances in techniques and development (such as complexity / difficulty in meeting requirements, percent proven technology, lack of work on similar projects, special resources required, operating environment, theoretical analysis required, and degree of difference from existing technology) could disrupt the project.
State-of-the-art advances, slow progress in		x			Slower progress than expected in making advances could disrupt the project.
State-of-the-art field failures				x	Field failures of state-of-the-art equipment types that were assumed to be ready for incorporation into the project could cause technical difficulties.
Survivability		x			New requirements for nuclear hardening, chemical survivability, and so on, might require revised planning to meet original or new goals.
Testing, extrapolation requirements				x	The need for extensive extrapolation using field test results could hamper the assessment of the project under actual deployment conditions.
Testing, facility compatibility			x		Not having suitable test facilities available during the required time frame could cause schedule delays.

Table B-1—*Continued*

Risk	Cost	Project	Schedule	Technical	Comments
Testing, incomplete or delayed support package for			x		Without an adequate test support package on site and ready to support the scheduled test, it might be possible to start testing, but the chances of continuing on schedule would be low.
Testing, inconsistencies				x	Inconsistent field test results could cause increased technical risk and require retesting.
Testing, safety				x	Problems could result from requirements that testing be nondestructive or that it not interfere with other activities.
Testing, security requirements			x		The testing of classified equipment could cause scheduling concerns associated with clearances, data transfer, and public interest.
Testing, unrealistic scenarios for		x			A subtle risk, particularly during development testing, and one that can have a lasting effect on the viability of a project, is testing to an unrealistic scenario. A realistic approach does not necessarily mean that stresses put on the system under test must duplicate those of actual service, because in most cases this is impractical. It does mean, however, that the test is planned to simulate conditions as closely as possible, with differences carefully documented.
Testing, weather	x		x		Weather-related occurrences could cause testing delays.
Threat changes	x		x		Possible changes could require alterations in schedule and performance objectives.
Uniquely harsh requirement				x	Existing design technology that differs significantly from that required for success of the new system could cause technical difficulties.

Table B-1—*Continued*

Risk	Cost	Project	Schedule	Technical	Comments
Vendor base	x	x	x		A shortage of qualified vendors can affect adequate price competition and a satisfactory supply quantity base.

BASIC PROBABILITY
CONCEPTS

This appendix serves as a very basic introduction to probability and statistical concepts that may be useful for risk analysis. It is by no means all inclusive, but rather may be thought of as a primer. The appendix contains three sections. The first section is an introduction to probability, centering on definitions and simple examples. The second section provides a summary of descriptive statistics, including a look at statistical confidence and confidence intervals, and explains probability density functions (PDFs) and cumulative density functions (CDFs) defining distributions such as the normal, uniform, and triangular, that are relevant to risk analysis. The third section discusses statistical independence, which is the prerequisite for the concept of expected value. Decision tree analysis is illustrated to show the merit of the expected value approach.

Probability

Probability is a concept used by many people every day. As an example, the weather forecaster predicts a 30 percent probability of rain. This means that, in the long run, rain is expected 30 days out of 100 when conditions are the same as they are at the time the forecast is made. For risk analysis, a statement might be made to the effect that the developmental stage of weapons system A has a 10 percent probability of a schedule (time) overrun. This is equivalent to saying that 10 percent of all developmental stages of weapons systems similar to A have had a schedule overrun in the past.

More formal definitions of probability follow.

   1. The quality or condition of being probable; likelihood. 2. A probable situation, condition, or event. 3. Math. A number expressing the likelihood of occurrence of a specific event, such as

the ratio of the number of experimental results that would produce the event to the total number of results considered possible. (*The American Heritage Dictionary* 1992)

In practical situations, probability is used as a vehicle in drawing inferences about unknown population characteristics. Additionally, . . . probability concepts can be used to give us an indication of how good these inferences are." (Pfaffenberger and Patterson 1977)

Many individuals think of probability in relation to gambling and games of chance such as card playing and dice throwing. They measure the probability of an event in terms of the odds against the event's happening. For example, throwing a pair of dice, illustrating the inverse relationship between probability and the odds against an event, results in 1 of 36 possible outcomes. These are illustrated in Figure C-1.

The probability of throwing a 10 is 3/36 or 0.083. That is, 3 out of the 36 possible outcomes result in a 10. The odds against throwing a 10 are 11 to 1. This is because the total number of possible non-10 outcomes, 33, is 11 times the number of outcomes, 3, which result in a 10.

Probability is a key quantitative measure associated with many risk assessment techniques. The above examples are simplistic but show how easy it is to comprehend probability concepts.

Descriptive Statistics, Confidence, and Distributions

Any group of numbers, such as a sample composed of quantitative evaluations, may be described with the following basic statistical parameters:

- Mean
- Median
- Range
- Mode
- Variance and standard deviation

These parameters enable the statistician to determine what level of confidence (or assurance) may be accorded to predictive statements about the entire population of numbers. The parameters also help determine where the sample lies in a possible statistical distribution. Conversely, a statistical distribution may be described by such parameters. A statistical distribution is basically just a way to describe which numbers will appear more often (or with a high probability) and which numbers will appear less often (or with a low probability). The following paragraphs define the

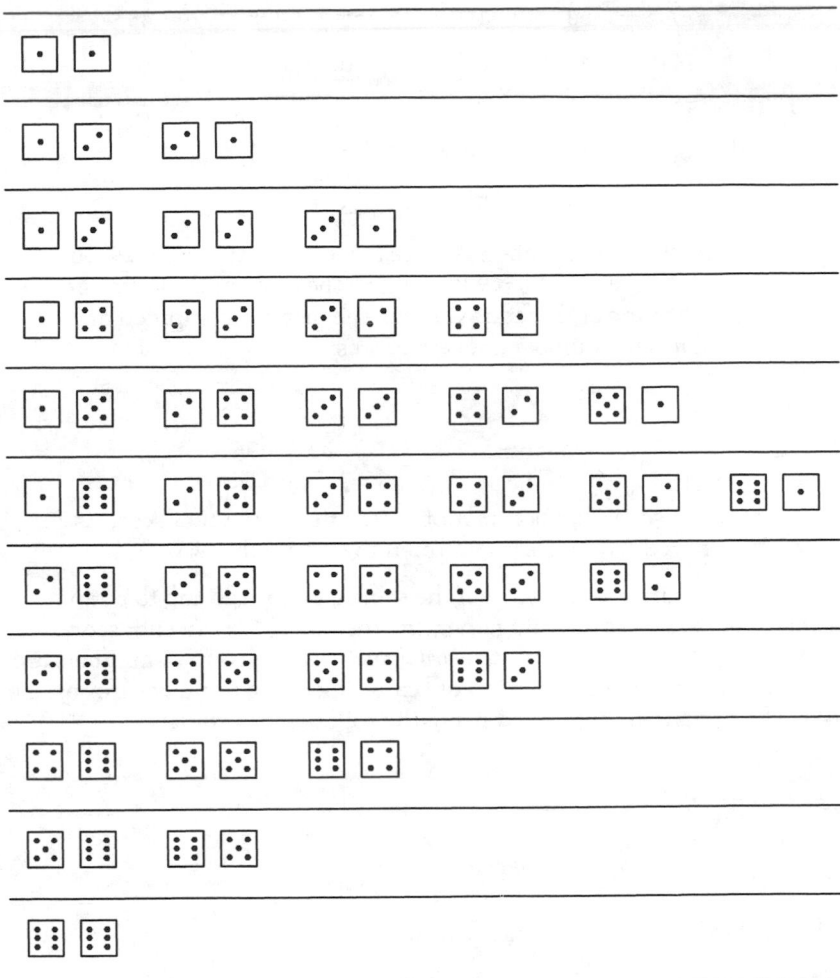

Figure C-1. Results of Variance in Throwing Dice

parameters in some detail and then discuss confidence levels, PDFs and CDFs, and the other relevant distributions applied in risk analysis.

For illustrative purposes, let the following numbers represent exam scores for an introductory statistics course:

75	60	100	65	80	45
25	45	60	90	60	40
50	70	55	10	95	70
85	20	70	65	90	90
65	80	70	55	70	

Let X_i represent these numbers, where i is indexed from 1 to 29. So $X_1 = 75$, $X_2 = 80$, $X_3 = 60$, ..., $X_{28} = 90$, $X_{29} = 55$. The *mean* of these numbers is nothing more than the arithmetic average. The mean is computed as follows, where n is the number of exam scores:

$$\text{Mean} = \frac{\sum_{i=1}^{n} X_i}{n} = \frac{1,855}{29} = 63.96$$

The *mode*, the score that occurs more often than any other score, is 70. The mode occurred five times (more often than any other score).

The *median* is the middle score if the scores are ranked top to bottom. Because there are 29 scores altogether, the median is the fifteenth score, which is a 65. The *variance* and *standard deviation* of a group of numbers are attempts to describe the dispersion or scattering of the numbers around the mean. The variance is computed using the following formula:

$$\text{Variance} = \frac{\sum_{i=1}^{n} X_i^2 - \frac{\left(\sum_{i=1}^{n} X_i\right)^2}{n}}{n-1}$$

For this example, the variance is as follows:

$$\frac{132,275 - \frac{1,855^2}{29}}{28} = 486.4$$

The *standard deviation* is the square root of the variance. The standard deviation has a more intuitive appeal than does the variance, because the standard deviation is the mathematical average variation of a value from the mean. For this example, the standard deviation is—

$$\sqrt{486.4} = 22.05$$

The *range* is the high score minus the low score. For this example, the range is $100 - 10 = 90$.

Many times when examining data, a *level of confidence* or *confidence interval* is used to indicate what certainty or faith is to be put in the sample being taken as representative of the entire population. Far and away, the most common measure is the confidence interval for the mean. A statement such as the following can be made about a particular sample mean:

The 95 percent confidence interval for the mean is 56 to 72.

Statistically, this statement means that of all the possible samples of this size taken from this population, 95 percent of the samples will have a mean between 56 and 72. It does not mean that 95 percent of all possible values that are sampled will fall between 56 and 72, which is the common, though faulty, interpretation of the statement.

Confidence intervals are determined by adding and subtracting some calculated value from the mean of the sample. Usually, but not always, this value is based on the standard deviation of the sample. As an example, if the population from which a sample is taken is determined to be normally distributed, and this was assumed in previous statements (this determination may be made based on the relative values of the mean, variance and standard deviation, mode, median, range, and other factors), then a 95 percent confidence interval for the population is calculated in this manner where $\overline{X}$ is the sample mean and σ is the standard deviation—

$$\overline{X} \pm 1.96\,\sigma$$

A 95 percent confidence interval for the mean is calculated in this manner—

$$\overline{X} \pm 1.96\,\frac{\sigma}{\sqrt{n}}$$

where $\dfrac{\sigma}{\sqrt{n}}$ is commonly referred to as the standard error.

How is the population determined to be normal (or normally distributed) in the first place? Similar groups of numbers have similar relationships between their respective parameters. These similarities help determine which distribution describes the entire population. Typical distributions for problems associated with risk are normal, uniform, triangular, and beta. (Discussion of the beta distribution is beyond the scope of this appendix. If further information on the beta distribution is needed, any of several statistics and operations research books can supply the information.)

For the normal distribution, 68.3 percent of all possible values lie within one standard deviation of the mean, 95.4 percent lie within two standard deviations, and 99.7 percent lie within three standard deviations. This is shown in the probability density function. The PDF gives the probability that certain values will occur. Figure C-2 illustrates a PDF for the exam scores example, assuming that the scores are from a normal distribution.

The normal distribution is, by strict definition, a continuous distribution. However, it is implied in Figure C-2 that fractional exam scores are possible—and of course it is not realistic in this example. A discussion of the differences between discrete and continuous distribution is beyond the scope of this appendix, and because the example is meant to be used only for illustrative purposes, this finer point of statistics will be ignored. It is also implied in Figure C-2 that extra credit is given because scores exceeding 100 are possible, and this could certainly be within the realm of the example. The most important distinction of the normal distribution PDF is the bell shape of the curve. This shape is the most definitive characteristic of any PDF.

The cumulative density function is the arithmetic summation of the PDF. In other words, the CDF gives the probability value (or any value less than the value) that will occur. The shape of the various distribution CDFs are distinctive, and the CDF is merely another way of illustrating the distribution. Figure C-3 illustrates a typical CDF for normally distributed values, in this case the exam scores example.

The uniform distribution is used to describe a set of values where every value has an equal probability of occurrence. Returning once again to the exam scores example, one might hypothesize that all possible scores (1 through 100+) have an equal probability of occurrence: 0.01. The PDF for this is illustrated in Figure C-4. Figure C-5 illustrates the uniform CDF.

The triangular distribution is used often in risk analysis situations to describe the most optimistic, most likely, and most pessimistic durations of some event or activity. The PDF of the triangular distribution, illustrated in Figure C-6, is not necessarily symmetric. Indeed, often the triangular distribution is purposely asymmetric or skewed to the right to reflect the possibility of very long time durations. These long durations are less likely to occur but do happen occasionally. Figure C-6 shows that the most likely production time for a widget wing is 8 days. Clearly, the average is skewed to the right and is very close to 9.3 days. Hence, the triangular distribution, when skewed, has a mode and mean that are clearly different. Contrast this to the normal distribution, where the mode and mean are the same (as is the median).

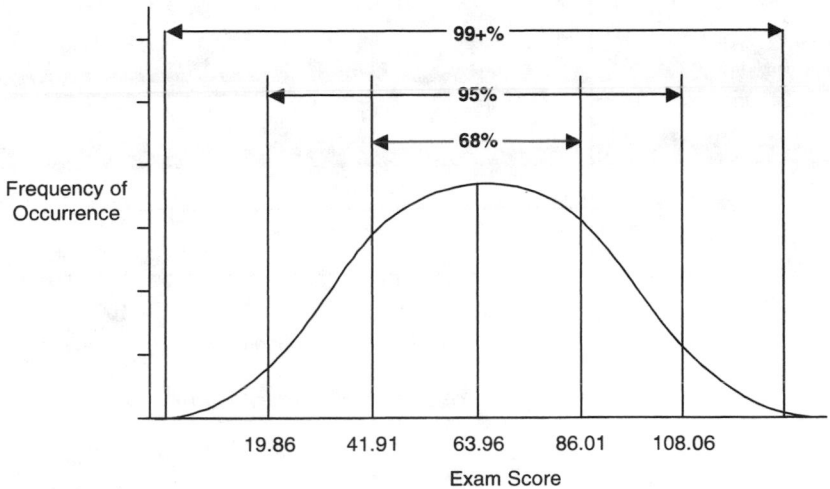

Figure C-2. PDF of a Normal Distribution

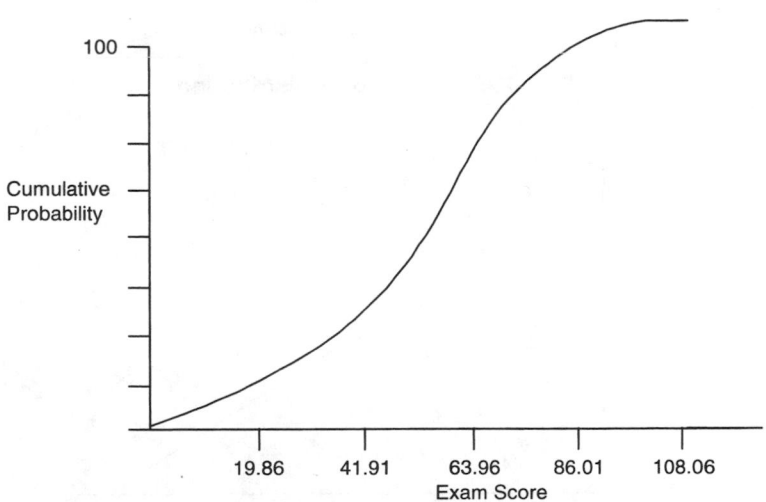

Figure C-3. CDF of a Normal Distribution

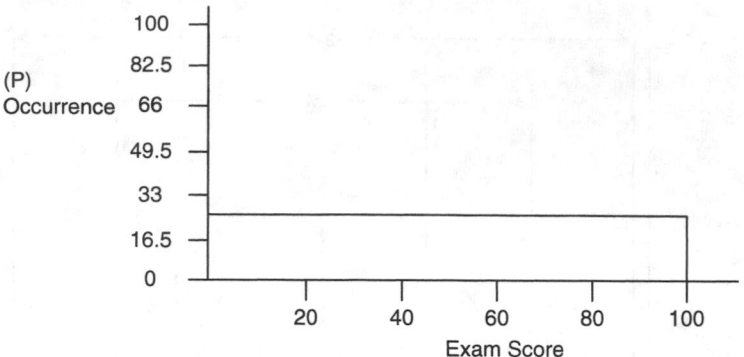

Figure C-4. PDF of a Uniform Distribution

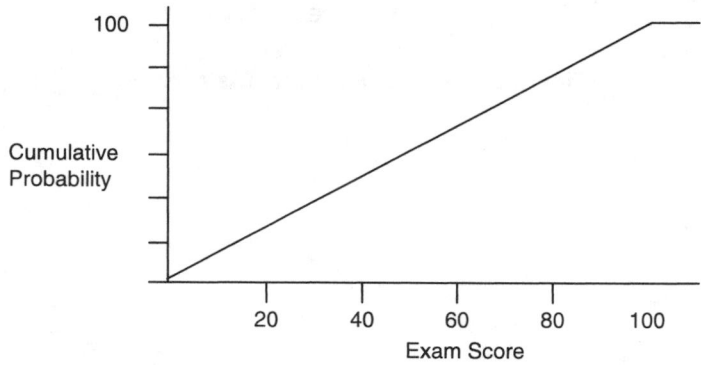

Figure C-5. CDF of a Uniform Distribution

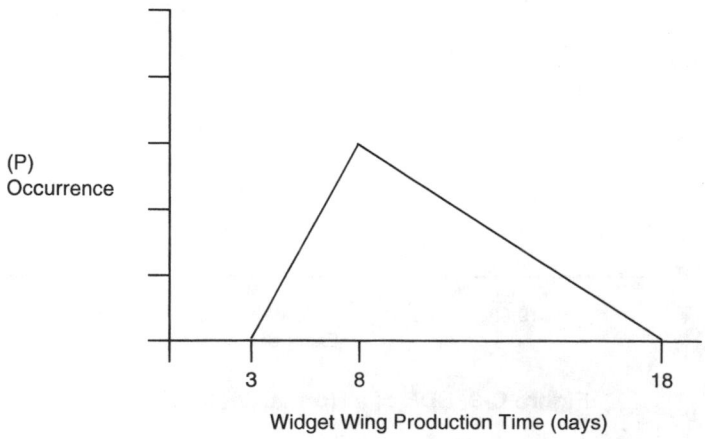

Figure C-6. PDF of a Triangular Distribution

Independence, Expected Value, and Decision Tree Analysis

Statistical independence is an important concept on which a good deal of methodologies are based. Most discussions of statistical independence begin with a tutorial on conditional probability, sample space, and event relationships. Rather than discuss these concepts, a more practical definition of statistical independence is presented: Two events are said to be independent if the occurrence of one is not related to the occurrence of the other. If events are occurring at random, they are independent; if events are not occurring at random, they are not independent. A set or group of possible events are said to be mutually exclusive and collectively exhaustive if they are all independent and the sum of their probabilities of occurrence is 1.0. This is the basic notion behind value.

To illustrate expected value, suppose that a simple game of chance can be played for $1. The bettor pays $1 and has a chance to win $50 or $2 or no money at all. The dollar amounts and probabilities are shown in Table C-1.

Table C-1. Expected Values Example

Amount Value	Probability of Winning	Expected Value
$50	0.01	$0.50
2	0.10	0.20
0	0.89	0.00
Totals	1.00	$0.70

The bettor would like to know, before actually paying $1, what the expected winnings are. The expected value of winnings is the sum of the winning amounts multiplied by their respective probability of occurrence:

$$(\$50)(0.01) + (\$2)(0.10) + (\$0)(0.89) =$$
$$\$0.50 + \$0.20 + \$0 =$$
$$\$0.70$$

Because the bettor can expect winnings on the average of only $0.70 but pays $1 to play the game, the net profit is a negative $0.30.

This is a very realistic example of gambling and risk. Most individuals, when forced to face this logic, would choose not to play. However, many would play. They are willing to accept the risk of losing $1 to take a chance at winning $50. These individuals are risk prone. The individuals who follow the basic logic of this example and do not play are risk averse.

The notion of expected value is a prerequisite for discussing decision tree analysis, which attempts to break down a series of events into smaller, simpler, and more manageable segments. Many similarities exist between decision tree analysis and more complicated forms of management and risk analysis, such as the Program Evaluation and Review Technique (PERT) and the critical path method (CPM). All three forms of analysis presume that a sequence of events can be broken down into smaller and smaller segments that more accurately represent reality.

Decision tree analysis helps the analyst break down a problem into various sectors or branches to simplify potential decision making. As an example, suppose a widget is being manufactured as follows: Either machine A or machine B can be used for the first step (of a two-step manufacturing process) with equal probability of 0.5. Either machine C or D can be used for the second step. Machine C is used 70 percent of the time if the widget was first processed with machine A and 40 percent of the time if the widget was first processed with machine B. The rest of the time, machine D is used for the second step. Decision tree analysis can help compute the probability of the widget's being produced by these various combinations (AC, AD, BC, BD). Figure C-7 illustrates the decision tree and the expected probability for each manufacturing process alternative.

Note that an alternative's probability is merely the product of the individual processes making up that alternative, because the individual processes are independent of each other. Note also that the sum of the probabilities for all of the four processing alternatives is 1.

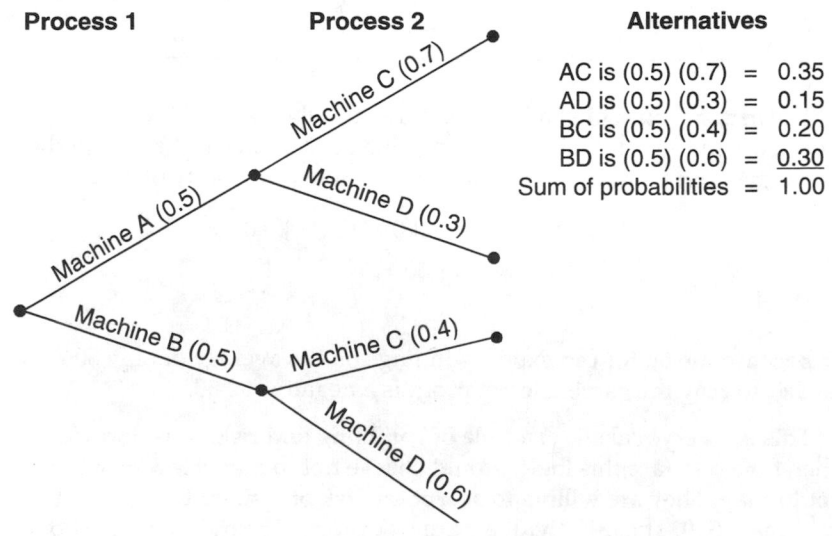

Process 1   **Process 2**   **Alternatives**

AC is (0.5) (0.7) = 0.35
AD is (0.5) (0.3) = 0.15
BC is (0.5) (0.4) = 0.20
BD is (0.5) (0.6) = 0.30
Sum of probabilities = 1.00

Machine C (0.7)
Machine A (0.5)
Machine D (0.3)
Machine B (0.5)
Machine C (0.4)
Machine D (0.6)

Figure C-7. Decision Tree Analysis

QUANTIFYING
EXPERT JUDGMENT

All risk assessment techniques or models share a common requirement: acquiring expert judgment as input. Inherent in judgment is a degree of uncertainty. When acquiring quantifiable expressions of judgment, the axioms of probability must not be violated:

- The probabilities of all possible events must sum to 1.

- The probability of any event, *P(A)*, must be a number greater than or equal to 0 and less than or equal to 1 ($0 \leq P(A) \leq 1$).

- The probability of joint events is the product of the probability that one event occurs and the probability that another event occurs, given that the first event has occurred, ($P(A) \times P(B|A)$). Under these circumstances, the events are termed dependent.

- When the probability of joint events' occurring is simply the product of the probabilities of each $P(A) \times P(B)$, the events are said to be independent. That is, the two events have nothing in common or can occur simultaneously.

The challenge for the analyst is to obtain expert judgment, which is qualitative by nature, in the areas of cost, schedule, and technical performance. Next, the analyst must convert that judgment into a quantitative form so that the results can be depicted in the form of a probability density function (PDF), which serves as input to the various risk models. (This is necessary only when a quantitative model has been selected.)

A PDF is a smooth line or curve, as shown in Figure D-1. The PDF of a random variable, *x*, is a listing of the various values of *x* with a corresponding probability associated with each value of *x*. In this example,

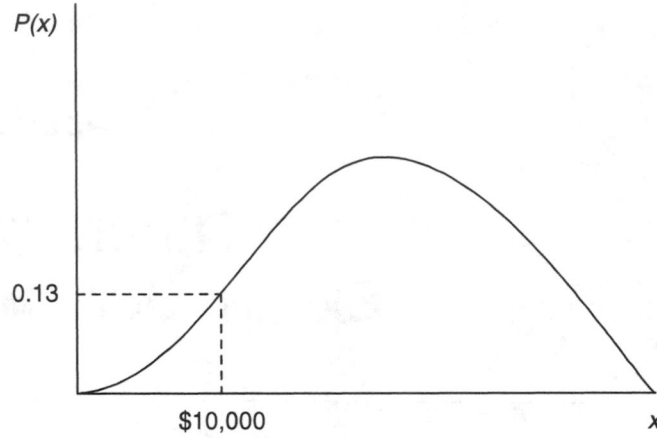

Figure D-1. Probability Density Function

x would be a cost, schedule, or performance value. Note that the total area under the curve equals 1.

In Figure D-1, the random variable x might represent a hardware system cost, where the probability of the system costing $10,000 is 0.13.

Several methods can be used to convert qualitative judgment into quantitative probability distributions. The remainder of this appendix focuses on a few of the most popular, practical, and accurate techniques for doing so, chosen because they are relatively simple and easy to master. This factor is of paramount importance, because in most cases, the analyst performing this task will have neither the time nor the knowledge of the advanced probability concepts required to perform more complex techniques. Those interested in more exotic, complex techniques are referred to "Sources of Additional Information" at the end of this appendix.

The following techniques are discussed in this appendix: diagrammatic, direct, betting, modified Churchman-Ackoff, and Delphi.

Description of Techniques

Diagrammatic

Many analysts prefer the diagrammatic method as a way of capturing and representing an expert's judgment. This method describes an expert's uncertainty by presenting the expert with a range of PDF diagrams and having the expert select the shape of the PDF that most accurately reflects the schedule, cost, or technical parameter in question. Using this method, the analyst can ascertain whether the PDF is symmetric or skewed, the degree of variability, and so on. For example, if the expert believes that there is a great amount of risk associated with completing an activity within a certain period of time, a PDF skewed to the right may be selected. Likewise, activities with little risk may be skewed to the left. If the expert believes that each value over a given range is equally likely to occur, a uniform distribution may be most appropriate. The analyst and the expert, working together, can select the PDF that most accurately reflects the schedule, cost, or technical item in question.

The diagrammatic method of obtaining PDFs is applicable when the expert has a sound understanding of probability concepts and can merge that understanding with his or her understanding of the parameters in question. In this way, the expert can accurately identify the appropriate PDFs.

Direct

The direct method is used to obtain subjective probability distributions by asking the expert to assign probabilities to a given range of values. This method of obtaining PDFs is applicable (1) when questions can be phrased to the respondents in such a way that no confusion is likely to exist in the respondents' mind and (2) when the results will not violate the axioms of probability. The direct method is applicable when time or resource constraints do not allow for more complex, resource-intensive methods.

By applying the direct method, the analyst defines a relevant range and discrete intervals for the parameters for constructing the PDF. For example, the analyst might define the relevant time duration for a project activity (test of a piece of equipment) to be between 0 and 27 days. The analyst then breaks down this relevant range into intervals, say of 4 days. The resulting formulation would be as follows:

0–3 days	16–19 days
4–7 days	20–23 days
8–11 days	24–27 days
12–15 days	

Given these intervals over the relevant range, the analyst then queries the expert to assign relative probabilities to each range. From this, the form of the PDF could be identified. It is imperative that the axioms of probability not be violated.

In addition to the application already described, the analyst could request that the expert provide a lowest possible value, a most likely value, and a highest possible value. The analyst then makes an assumption about the form of the density function. That is, is the PDF normal, uniform, triangular, or beta?

Betting

One method of phrasing questions to experts in order to obtain probabilities for ranges of values (cost and schedule) states the problem in terms of betting. A form of this method helps the expert (assessor) assess probabilities of events that are in accordance with his or her judgment (Winkler 1967). The assumption with this method is that the judgment of the expert may be fully represented by a probability distribution, $f(x)$, of a random variable, x. This method offers the expert a series of bets.

Under ideal circumstances, the bets are actual, not hypothetical. That is, in each case the winner of the bet is determined and the amount of money involved actually changes hands. (This is not feasible, however, because betting is illegal.) In each case, the expert must choose between two bets (the expert may not refrain from betting). The expert must choose between a bet with a fixed probability of winning (q) and of losing $(1 - q)$, and a bet dependent on whether some event (a particular project activity duration range or cost range) occurs (E). The bet can be depicted as follows:

Bet 1a
- Win \$A if event E occurs.
- Lose \$B if event E does not occur.

Bet 1b
- Win \$A with probability of q.
- Lose \$B with probability of $1 - q$.

The expected values of bets 1a and 1b to the expert are respectively $Ap + Bp = B$ and $Aq + Bq = B$, where p is the probability of the occurrence of event E. The following inferences may be drawn from the expert's decision: if bet 1a is chosen, $Ap + Bp - B \geq Aq + Bq - B$, so $p \geq q$; likewise, if 1b is selected, $p \leq q$.

By repeating the procedure, varying the value of q, the probability of event E can be ascertained. It is the point at which the expert is indifferent to both bets 1a and 1b that $p = q$. The degree of precision depends on the number of bets and the incremental changes of the value of q. To avoid the problem of a large number of bets to obtain p is to assess the probabilities by using direct interrogation and then using the betting situation as a check on the assumed probabilities.

To complete a PDF, the analyst repeats this procedure over a relevant range of interval values. The analyst then plots the points at the center of the range for each event and smooths in a curve so that the area under it equals 1, as in Figure D-2. The analyst must ensure that all relevant axioms of probability are maintained.

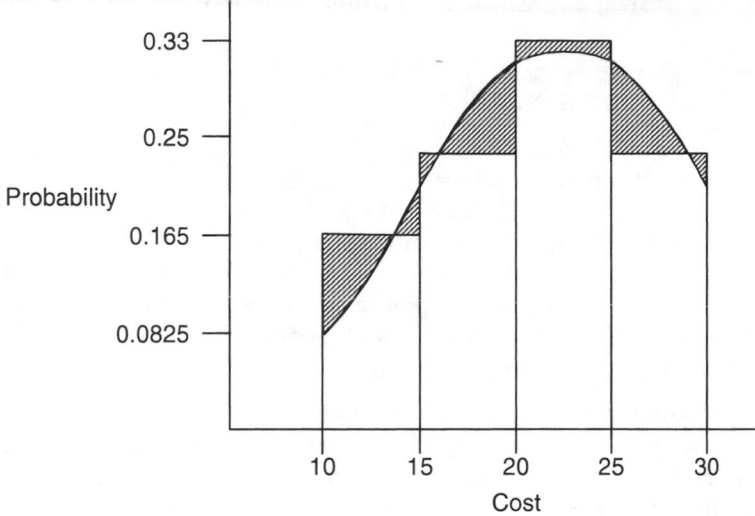

Figure D-2. Fitting a Curve to Expert Judgment

When questioned one way, many people are likely to make probability statements that are inconsistent with what they will say when questioned in another equivalent way, especially when they are asked for direct assignment of probabilities. As the number of events increases, so does the difficulty of assigning direct probabilities. When this is a problem, the betting method is most appropriate.

To apply the betting technique, select one interval for the relevant range to demonstrate how this method can be used to obtain probability estimates and, hence, PDFs. The bet is established as follows:

Bet 1a
- Win $10,000 if cost is between $15,100 and $20,000.
- Lose $5,000 if cost is not between $15,100 and $20,000.

Bet 1b
- Win $10,000 with probability of q.
- Lose $5,000 with probability of $1 - q$.

The value of q is established initially, and the expert is asked which of the two bets he or she would take.

The value of q is then varied systematically (either increased or decreased). The point at which the expert is indifferent between the two bets (with the associated q value) provides the probability of the cost's being between $15,100 and $20,000. This process is repeated for each interval, and the results create the PDF associated with the cost of that particular project event.

Modified Churchman-Ackoff

Another way to ascertain PDFs for cost, schedule, or performance parameters is the modified Churchman-Ackoff method (Churchman-Ackoff 1951). This technique was developed as a way to order events in terms of likelihood. The technique was modified so that after the event likelihoods were ordered, relative probabilities could be assigned to the events and, finally, PDFs could be developed. For relevancy, events are defined as range values for cost, schedule, or performance (activity durations) relating to the outcome of a specific activity in a project.

The modified Churchman-Ackoff technique is most appropriate when there is one expert and that expert has a thorough understanding of the relative ranking of cost and schedule ranges and a limited understanding of probability concepts. The remainder of this section is extracted and modified from the *Compendium on Risk Analysis Techniques* (Atzinger 1972). Note that although the mathematical calculations appear to make this a precise technique, it is still an approximation of an expert's judgment and should not be interpreted to be more exact than other similar techniques.

The first step in applying the modified Churchman-Ackoff technique is to define the relevant range of values. That is, the end points along a range of values with 0 probability of occurrence must be specified. These values can be any low and high values the expert specifies as having 0 probability of occurrence. Next, ranges of individual values within the relevant range must be determined. These ranges of values, which will form the set of comparative values for this technique, are specified by the following approach:

Step 1   Start with the low value in the relevant range.

Step 2   Progress upward on the scale of values until the expert is able to state a simple preference regarding the relative probabilities of occurrence of the two characteristic values. If the expert is able to voice a belief that one value has either a greater or lesser chance of occurring that the other of the two values, then it is inferred that the expert is able to discriminate between the two values.

Step 3   Using the higher of the two previously specified scale values as a new basis, repeat Step 2 to determine the next value on the scale.

Step 4   Repeat Steps 2 and 3 until the high end-point value of the range of parameter values is approached.

Using this procedure for the duration required to successfully test a piece of equipment successfully may yield the results shown in Table D-1.

Table D-1. Characteristic Values for Equipment Test Durations

Value	Duration (days)
0_1	0–3
0_2	4–7
0_3	8–11
0_4	12–15
0_5	16–19
0_6	20–23
0_7	24–27

The descending order of probability or occurrence can be determined by applying the following paired comparison method. Ask the expert to compare, one at a time, the first interval value (0_1) of the set to each of the other values $(0_2, 0_3,$ and so on), stating a preference for that value in each group of two values that he or she believes has the greater chance of occurring (denoting a greater probability of occurrence by >, an equal chance by =, and a lesser chance by <). The following hypothetical preference relationships could result for a set of seven values $(0_1 < 0_2, 0_1 < 0_3, 0_1 < 0_4, 0_1 < 0_5, 0_1 < 0_6, 0_1 < 0_7)$.

Next, ask the expert to compare, one at a time, the second interval value (0_2) of the set to each of the other interval values succeeding it in the set (that is, $0_3, 0_4,$ and so on). The following preference relationships might result $(0_2 < 0_3, 0_2 < 0_4, 0_2 < 0_5, 0_2 < 0_6, 0_2 < 0_7)$. Continue this process until all values have been compared.

Now total the number of times a given value was preferred over other values. The results for this procedure are listed in Table D-2.

List the values in descending order of simple ordinal probability preference, and change the symbols for each value from 0_i to X_j as shown in Table D-3.

Table D-2. Summary of Preference Relationships

Value	Times
0_4	6
0_3	5
0_5	4
0_2	3
0_6	2
0_1	0
0_7	0

Table D-3. Transformation

Characteristic	Value (days)	Reference Rank	New Symbol
0–3	0_4	1	X_1
4–7	0_3	2	X_2
8–11	0_5	3	X_3
12–15	0_2	4	X_4
16–19	0_6	5	X_5
20–23	0_1	6	X_6
24–27	0_7	7	X_7

Arbitrarily assign a rating of 100 points to the characteristic value with the highest subjective probability (that is, X_1). Then, as in the first step, question the expert regarding the relative chance of occurrence of each of the other values on the ordinal scale in Table D-3 with respect to the value at the top of the scale. Assigning X_1 a rating of 100 points, the expert is first interrogated as to his or her feeling of the relative chance of occurrence of the second highest scale value (X_2), with respect to X_1. Does it have a 25, 60, 70, or 80 percent chance? As much chance of realization as X_1? The relative probability rating, based on 100 points, (that is, 100 percent as much chance) than will be posted for X_2.

Next, question the expert about the relative chance of occurrence of the next highest scale (X_3), first with respect to the most preferred value (X_1) and then with respect to the second most preferred scale value (X_2). The resulting numerical ratings should occur. For example, if the expert decides that X_2 has 80 percent as much chance of occurring as does X_1, and that X_3 has 50 percent as much chance as X_1, and 62.5 percent as much chance as X_2, the ratings would be $X_1 = 100$ points, $X_2 = 80$ points, and $X_3 = 50$ points.

This process continues for each successively lower interval value on the ordinal scale as shown in Table D-3. Determine the relative number of points to be accorded each value with respect to the top scale and with respect to all other values down the scale that are above the characteristic value in question.

If there are minor disparities between relative probability ratings for a given value, the average of all such ratings for that characteristic value might be computed. For example, X_4 might be determined to be 30 percent as probable as X_1, 25 percent as probable as X_2, and 50 percent as probable as X_3. The three absolute ratings for X_4 are thus inferred to be 30, 20, and 25 points, respectively. The average of these ratings is 25. However, before averaging such figures, it might be beneficial to have the expert reevaluate the relative ratings for X_4 with respect to X_1, X_2, and X_5.

As a result of this process, the relative probability values shown in Table D-4 might be attained.

Table D-4. Relative Probability Ratings

Value	Probability Points
RX_1	100
RX_2	80
RX_3	50
RX_4	25
RX_5	10
RX_6	0
RX_7	0

Finally, the scale of relative probability values can be converted directly into a scale of actual probability density values by having $P(X_1)$ equal the actual subjective probability or occurrence of the highest value. Then $P(X_2)$ is defined as—

$$\frac{RX_2}{RX_1}\left[P(X_1)\right]$$

Similarly, for i = 2, 3, . . . 7, $P(X_i)$ is defined as—

$$\frac{RX_i}{RX_1}\left[P(X_1)\right]$$

Assuming that the independent characteristic values evaluated represent all possible values attainable by the component characteristic, the respective probabilities must total 1 (that is, $P(X_1) + P(X_2) + P(X_3) + P(X_4) + P(X_5) + P(X_6) + P(X_7) = 1$). Substituting the expressions for $P(X_i)$, $i = 2, . . . 7$, it follows that—

$$P(X_1) + \frac{RX_2}{RX_1}\left[P(X_1)\right] + \frac{RX_3}{RX_1}\left[P(X_1)\right] + \frac{RX_4}{RX_1}\left[P(X_1)\right]$$

$$+ \frac{RX_5}{RX_1}\left[P(X_1)\right] + \frac{RX_6}{RX_1}\left[P(X_1)\right] + \frac{RX_7}{RX_1}\left[P(X_1)\right] = 1$$

Solving this equation for $P(X_1)$, the remaining $P(X_i)$, $i = 2, . . . 7$ can be determined using the relationship—

$$P(X_1) = \frac{RX_i}{RX_j}\left[P(X_1)\right]$$

As an illustration, consider the relative probability ratings in Table D-4. Using the values, the preceding equation is given by—

$$P(X_1) + \frac{80}{100}P(X_1) + \frac{50}{100}P(X_1)$$

$$+ \frac{25}{100}P(X_1) + \frac{10}{100}P(X_1) = 1$$

Solving this equation, $P(X_1) = 0.377$.

This value can be used to determine the remaining probabilities as follows:

$$P(X_2) = \frac{RX_2}{RX_1}P(X_1) = 0.80\ (0.377) = 0.301$$

$$P(X_3) = \frac{RX_3}{RX_1}P(X_1) = 0.50\ (0.377) = 0.189$$

$$P(X_4) = \frac{RX_4}{RX_1}P(X_1) = 0.25\ (0.377) = 0.095$$

$$P(X_5) = \frac{RX_5}{RX_1} P(X_1) = 0.10 \, (0.377) = 0.038$$

$$P(X_6) = \frac{RX_6}{RX_1} P(X_1) = 0 \, (0.377) = 0$$

$$P(X_7) = \frac{RX_7}{RX_1} P(X_1) = 0 \, (0.377) = 0$$

The resulting probability density appears in Table D-5.

Table D-5. Probability Density

Component Characteristic Value	Probability
X_1	0.377
X_2	0.301
X_3	0.189
X_4	0.095
X_5	0.038
X_6	0.000
X_7	0.000
Total	1.000

Delphi

In many cases, expert judgment does not reside solely with one individual but is spread among multiple experts. Committee approaches to obtaining a group assessment have been found to contain problems relating to interpersonal pressures to a degree that caused researchers at the RAND Corporation to devise a method known as the Delphi technique to avoid the pressures.

The Delphi technique has become well known in management circles, but it is subject to misconception. Too often, the term is used to identify a committee or multiple interview process, and these do not share the advantages of the Delphi approach. The Delphi technique has been extended in recent years to cover a wide variety of types of group interaction. The technique can be used for group estimation, that is, the use of a group of knowledgeable individuals to arrive at an estimate of an uncertain quantity. The quantity can be a cost, a time period associated with an event, or a performance level. There are a number of situations for which the Delphi technique is most appropriate:

- The problem does not lend itself to precise analytical techniques but can benefit from subjective judgments on a collective basis.

- The individuals needed to contribute to the examination of a broad or complex problem have no history of adequate communication and may represent diverse backgrounds with respect to experience or expertise.

- More individuals are needed than can effectively interact in a face-to-face exchange.

- Time and cost make frequent group meetings infeasible.

- The efficiency of face-to-face meetings can be increased by a supplemental group communication process.

- Disagreements among individuals are so severe or politically unpalatable that the communication process must be refereed or anonymity ensured.

- The heterogeneity of the participants must be preserved to ensure validity of the results, that is, avoidance of domination by quantity or by strength of personality ("bandwagon effect").

The Delphi technique differs from other methods of obtaining a group opinion, because it physically separates the group's members from one another to reduce irrelevant interpersonal influences. Properly carried out, the technique is facilitated by an analyst obtaining each panel member's opinion and each member's reason for the opinion. The analyst then reduces the opinions and reasons to standard statements to preserve anonymity. The analyst then shows the panel member the aggregated opinions of the other panel members in statistical terms. The analyst provides each panel member with the reasons justifying opinions that differ from the member's, and requests revaluation and further substantiation. This iterative feedback continues until no further substantial change results. At this point, the moderator takes the final individual opinions and computes a set of median values to represent the group opinion. The median value, rather than the average, is used as a central estimate to prevent the estimate from being overly influenced by extreme individual values.

One technique that holds much promise as a means of capturing expert judgment is "expert support systems." Ideally, the expert support system would lead the expert(s) through a series of parameter-specific questions (cost and schedule, and possibly performance) and generate PDFs based on the responses.

Resource Requirements

The effort required to conduct expert interviews and generate appropriate PDFs is time intensive. Much time is spent by the analyst with each expert acquiring and quantifying the expert's expertise. How long it takes to accomplish this task is predicated on the number of PDFs needed (based on the number of activities required as model input and whether cost, schedule, and technical distributions are required). The methods described are basically manual with computer resources not a necessity. However, as the techniques become more complex and expert support systems to accomplish the tasks are developed, computer resources required will escalate dramatically.

Reliability

The reliability of the PDFs obtained through these techniques is affected by several factors. Foremost is the degree to which the so-called expert is qualified. The better the understanding the expert has of the parameter being modeled, the more reliable the resulting PDFs will be. The burden also falls on the analyst to select the technique most appropriate for obtaining PDFs. For example, if expertise resides with more than one person, the Delphi technique would produce much more reliable PDFs than would a direct method of asking only one expert. Likewise, it would be inappropriate to ask an expert with little understanding of probability concepts to select a PDF from a visual list of options. Under these circumstances, the modified Churchman-Ackoff method or a betting technique would most likely result in more reliable PDFs. In summary, much of the reliability of the PDFs is predicated on the technique selected by the analyst for constructing them. Therefore, it is important that the analyst know when each technique is most appropriate, given the unique circumstances of that specific organization.

Sources of
Additional Information

Atzinger, E.M., et al. *Compendium on Risk Analysis Techniques*. AD 746245, LD 28463. Aberdeen Proving Ground, Md.: DARCOM Material Systems Analysis Activity, 1972.

Brown, R.V., A.S.S. Kahr, and C. Peterson. *Decision Analysis for the Manager*. New York: Holt, Rinehart & Winston, 1974.

Churchman, C. West, and Russell L. Ackoff. "Methods of Inquiry: An Introduction to Philosophy and Scientific Method." *Philosophy and Phenomenological Research* 12 (1951): 149–50.

Dalkey, Norman C. *The Delphi Method: An Experimental Study of Group Opinion*. Santa Monica, Calif.: The RAND Corp., 1968.

DeGroot, M.H. *Optimal Statistical Decisions*. New York: McGraw-Hill, 1970.

Linstone, H.A., and M. Turoff. *The Delphi Method: Techniques and Applications*. Reading, Mass.: Addison-Wesley, 1975.

Singleton, W.T., and J. Houden. *Risk and Decision*. New York: John Wiley & Sons Ltd., 1987.

Winkler, R.L. "Probabilistic Prediction: Some Experimental Results." *Journal of the American Statistical Association* 66, (1971): 675–685.

———. "The Quantification of Judgment: Some Methodological Suggestions." *Journal of the American Statistical Association* 62 (1967): 1105–1120.

SPECIAL NOTES ON SOFTWARE RISK

Although the techniques and processes discussed in *Risk Management: Concepts and Guidance* apply to software, they do not address some of the peculiarities that are a part of software development. Software has a tendency to change dramatically during the development cycle when compared with hardware. This appendix suggests some useful actions in managing software development efforts. Additional information can be obtained from Chapter 20 of the *DSMC Systems Engineering Management Guide* (1990).

One of the most effective risk management (handling) techniques for software is establishing a formal software quality assurance program early in the development cycle. The program should establish a team of experts whose charter is to explicitly look at issues that will ensure a reliable product in a reasonable time and at a reasonable cost. Some of the questions the team must answer include the following:

- Is independent verification and validation warranted?
- Is the development environment adequate (tool sets, compiler)?
- Is the higher-order language selection appropriate?
- Are the requirements clearly stated?
- Will rapid prototyping be used?
- Has the software approach been baselined?
- Has the testing philosophy been established?
- Has the development philosophy been established?

Addressing these issues early in the development cycle will help avoid surprises. The basic process for risk management still applies to software— plan, assess, analyze, and handle. Tables E-1 to E-5, which are extracts from government pamphlets (AFSC 1985, 1987), may prove useful in quantifying software risk.

Table E-1. Quantification of Probability and Impact of Technical Drivers

	Magnitude		
Technical Drivers	**Low (0.0–0.3)**	**Medium (0.4–0.5)**	**High (0.6–1.0)**
Requirements			
Complexity	Simple or easily allocatable	Moderate, can be allocated	Significant or difficult to allocate
Size	Small or easily broken down into work units	Medium or can be broken down into work units	Large or cannot be broken down into work loads
Stability	Little or no change to established baseline	Some change in baseline expected	Rapidly changing or no baseline
Reliability and maintainability	Allocatable to hardware and software components	Requirements can be defined	Can be addressed only at the total system level
Constraints			
Computer resources	Mature, growth capacity within design, flexible	Available, some growth capacity	New development, no growth capacity, inflexible
Personnel	Available, in place, experienced, stable	Available, but not in place, some experience	High turnover, little or no experience, not available
Standards	Appropriately tailored for application	Some tailoring, all not reviewed for applicability	No tailoring, none applied to the contract
Buyer-furnished equipment and property	Meets requirements, available	May meet requirements, uncertain availability	Not compatible with system requirements, unavailable

Table E-1—*Continued*

Technical Drivers	Magnitude		
	Low (0.0–0.3)	**Medium** (0.4–0.5)	**High** (0.6–1.0)
Constraints—*Continued*			
Environment	Little or no effect on design	Some effect on design	Major effect on design
Technology			
Language	Mature, approved high-order language used	Approved or nonapproved high-order language	Significant use of assembly language
Hardware	Mature, available	Some development or available	Total new development
Tools	Documented, validated, in place	Available, validated, some development	Unvalidated, proprietary, major development
Data rights	Fully compatible with support and follow-on	Minor incompatibilities support and follow-on	Incompatible with support and follow-on
Experience	Greater than 3 to 5 years	Less than 3 to 5 years	Little or none
Developmental Approach			
Prototypes and reuse	Used, documented sufficiently for use	Some use and documentation	No use and/or no documentation
Documentation	Correct and available	Some deficiencies, available	Nonexistent
Environment	In place, validated, experience with use	Minor modifications, tools available	Major development effort

Table E-1—*Continued*

Technical Drivers	Magnitude		
	Low (0.0–0.3)	Medium (0.4–0.5)	High (0.6–1.0)
Developmental Approach—*Continued*			
Management approach	Existing product and process controls	Product and process controls need enhancement	Weak or nonexistent
Integration	Internal and external controls in place	Internal or external controls not in place	Weak or nonexistent
Impact	Minimal-to-small reduction in technical performance	Some reduction in technical performance	Significant degradation to non-achievement of technical performance

Table E-2. Quantification of Probability and Impact of Operational Drivers

Operational Drivers	Magnitude		
	Low (0.0–0.3)	Medium (0.4–0.5)	High (0.6–1.0)
User Perspective			
Requirements	Compatible with user environment	Some incompatibilities	Major incompatibilities with operations concepts
Stability	Little or no change	Some controlled change	Uncontrolled change
Test environment	Representative of the user environment	Some aspects are not representative	Major disconnects with user environment

Table E-2—*Continued*

Operational Drivers	Magnitude		
	Low (0.0–0.3)	Medium (0.4–0.5)	High (0.6–1.0)
User Perspective—*Continued*			
Test results	Test errors/ failures are correctable	Some errors/ failures are not correctable before implementation	Major corrections necessary
Quantification	Primarily objective	Some subjectivity	Primarily subjective
Technical Performance			
Usability	User friendly	Mildly unfriendly	User unfriendly
Reliability	Predictable performance	Some aspects unpredictable	Unpredictable
Flexibility	Adaptable with threat	Some aspects not adaptable	Critical functions not adaptable
Supportability	Timely incorporation	Response times inconsistent with need	Unresponsive
Integrity	Responsive to update	Hidden linkages, controlled access	Insecure
Performance Envelope			
Adequacy	Full compatibility	Some limitations	Inadequate
Expandability	Easily expanded	Can be expanded	No expansion
Enhancements	Timely incorporation	Some lag	Major delays
Threat	Responsive to change	Cannot respond to some changes	Unresponsive

Table E-2—*Continued*

	Magnitude		
Operational Drivers	**Low (0.0–0.3)**	**Medium (0.4–0.5)**	**High (0.6–1.0)**
Impact	Full mission capability	Some limitations on mission performance	Severe performance limitations

Table E-3. Quantification of Probability and Impact of Support Drivers

	Magnitude		
Support Drivers	**Low (0.0–0.3)**	**Medium (0.4–0.5)**	**High (0.6–1.0)**
Design			
Complexity	Structurally maintainable	Certain aspects difficult	Extremely difficult to maintain
Documentation	Adequate	Some deficiencies	Inadequate
Completeness	Few additional support requirements	Some support requirements	Extensive support requirements
Configuration management	Sufficient, in place	Some shortfalls	Insufficient
Stability	Little or no change	Moderate, controlled change	Rapid or uncontrolled change
Responsibilities			
Management	Defined, assigned responsibilities	Some roles and mission issues	Undefined or unassigned
Configuration management	Single-point control	Defined control points	Multiple control points
Technical management	Consistent with operational needs	Some inconsistencies	Major inconsistencies

Table E-3—*Continued*

Support Drivers	Magnitude		
	Low (0.0–0.3)	**Medium** (0.4–0.5)	**High** (0.6–1.0)
Responsibilities—*Continued*			
Change implementation	Responsive to user needs	Acceptable delays	Nonresponsive to user needs
Tools and Management			
Facilities	In place, little change	In place, some modification	Nonexistent or extensive change
Software tools	Delivered, certified, sufficient	Some resolvable concerns	Not delivered, certified, or sufficient
Computer hardware	Compatible with operations system	Minor incompatibilities	Major incompatibilities
Production	Sufficient for distributed units	Some capacity questions	Insufficient
Distribution	Controlled, responsive	Minor response concerns	Uncontrolled or nonresponsive
Supportability			
Changes	Within projections	Slight deviations	Major deviations
Operational interfaces	Defined, controlled	Some hidden linkages	Extensive linkages
Personnel	In place, sufficient experience	Minor discipline mixed concerns	Significant concerns
Release cycle	Responsive to user requirements	Minor incompatibilities	Nonresponsive to user needs
Procedures	In place, adequate	Some concerns	Nonexistent or inadequate

Table E-3—*Continued*

	Magnitude		
Support Drivers	**Low** (0.0–0.3)	**Medium** (0.4–0.5)	**High** (0.6–1.0)
Impact	Responsive software support	Minor delays in software modifications	Nonresponsive or unsupportable software

Table E-4. Quantification of Probability and Impact of Cost Drivers

	Magnitude		
Cost Drivers	**Low** (0.0–0.3)	**Medium** (0.4–0.5)	**High** (0.6–1.0)
Requirements			
Size	Small, noncomplex, or easily broken down	Medium, moderate complexity, can be broken down	Large, highly complex, or cannot be broken down
Resource constraints	Little or no hardware-imposed constraints	Some hardware-imposed constraints	Significant hardware-imposed constraints
Application	Non-real-time, little system interdependency	Embedded, some system interdependency	Real-time, embedded, strong interdependency
Technology	Mature, existent, in-house experience	Existent, some in-house experience	New or new application, little experience
Requirements stability	Little or no change to established baseline	Some change in baseline expected	Rapidly changing or no baseline

Table E-4—*Continued*

Cost Drivers	Low (0.0–0.3)	Medium (0.4–0.5)	High (0.6–1.0)
Personnel			
Availability	In place, little turnover expected	Available, some turnover expected	High turnover, not available
Mix	Good mix of software disciplines	Some disciplines inappropriately represented	Some disciplines not represented
Experience	High experience ratio	Average experience ratio	Low experience ratio
Management engineering	Strong management approach	Good personnel management approach	Weak personnel management approach
Reusable Software			
Availability	Compatible with need dates	Delivery dates in question	Incompatible with need dates
Modifications	Little or no change	Some changes	Extensive changes
Language	Compatible with system requirements	Partial compatibility with requirements	Incompatible with system requirements
Rights	Compatible with competition requirements	Partial compatibility, some competition	Incompatible with concept, non-competitive
Certification	Verified performance, application compatible	Some application-compatible, some competition	Unverified, little test data available
Tools and Environment			
Facilities	Existent, little or no modification	Existent, some modification	Nonexistent, extensive changes

Table E-4—*Continued*

Cost Drivers	Low (0.0–0.3)	Medium (0.4–0.5)	High (0.6–1.0)
Tools and Environment—*Continued*			
Availability	In place, meets need dates	Some compatibility with need dates	Nonexistent, does not meet need dates
Rights	Compatible with development plans	Partial compatibility with development plans	Incompatible with development plans
Configuration management	Fully controlled	Some controls	No controls
Impact	Sufficient financial resources	Some shortage of financial resources, possible overrun	Significant financial shortages, budget overrun likely

Table E-5. Quantification of Probability and Impact of Schedule Drivers

Schedule Drivers	Magnitude		
	Low (0.0–0.3)	Medium (0.4–0.5)	High (0.6–1.0)
Resources			
Personnel	Good discipline mix in place	Some disciplines not available	Questionable mix and/or availability
Facilities	Existent, little or no modification	Existent, some modification	Nonexistent, extensive changes
Financial	Sufficient budget allocated	Some questionable allocations	Budget allocation in doubt

Table E-5—*Continued*

Schedule Drivers	Magnitude		
	Low (0.0–0.3)	**Medium** (0.4–0.5)	**High** (0.6–1.0)
Need Dates			
Threat	Verified projections	Some unstable aspects	Rapidly changing
Economic	Stable commitments	Some uncertain commitments	Unstable, fluctuating commitments
Political	Little projected sensitivity	Some limited sensitivity	Extreme sensitivity
Buyer-furnished equipment and property	Available, certified	Certification or delivery questions	No application evidence
Tools	In place, available	Some deliveries in question	Little or none
Technology			
Availability	In place	Baselined, some unknowns	Unknown, no baseline
Maturity	Application verified	Controllable change projected	Rapid or uncontrolled change
Experience	Extensive application	Some dependency on new technology	Incompatible with existing technology
Requirements			
Definition	Known, baselined	Baselined, some unknowns	Unknown, no baseline
Stability	Little or no change projected	Controllable change projected	Rapid or uncontrollable change
Complexity	Compatible with existing technology	Some dependency on new technology	Incompatible with existing technology

Table E-5—*Continued*

Schedule Drivers		Magnitude	
	Low (0.0–0.3)	Medium (0.4–0.5)	High (0.6–1.0)
Impact	Realistic achievable schedule	Possible slippage in implementation	Unachievable implementation

GLOSSARY

acceptance
Risk response strategy that prepares for and deals with the consequences of a risk, either actively (for example, by developing a contingency plan to execute if the risk event occurs) or passively (for example, by accepting a lower profit if some activities run over budget). *See also* avoidance *and* mitigation.

activity
Element of work that is required by the project, uses resources, and takes time to complete. Activities have expected durations, costs, and resource requirements and may be subdivided into tasks. *See also* task.

activity-on-arrow (AOA)
See arrow diagramming method.

activity-on-node (AON)
See precedence diagramming method.

amount at stake
Extent of positive or adverse consequences that could occur to the project if a specific risk, or series of risks, occurs. The potential value (positive or negative) associated with a risk. *See also* project risk.

analogous estimating
Using the actual duration or cost of a previous, similar activity as the basis for estimating the duration or cost of a present or future activity; a form of expert judgment.

arrow

In ADM, graphic presentation of an activity. The tail of the arrow represents the start of the activity; the head of the arrow represents the finish. Unless a time scale is used, the length of the arrow stem has no relation to the duration of the activity.

arrow diagramming method (ADM)

Network diagramming technique in which activities are represented by arrows. The tail of the arrow represents the start of the activity; the head of the arrow represents the finish of the activity. The length of the arrow does not represent the expected duration of the activity. Activities are connected at points called nodes (usually drawn as circles) to illustrate the sequence in which the activities are expected to be performed. *Also called* activity-on-arrow.

avoidance

Risk response strategy that eliminates the threat of a specific risk event, usually by eliminating its potential cause. The project management team can never eliminate all risk, but certain risk events often can be eliminated. *See also* acceptance *and* mitigation.

brainstorming

Problem-solving technique that can be used for planning purposes, risk identification, improvement efforts, and other project-related endeavors. Participants are invited to share their ideas in a group setting, where no disapproving verbal or nonverbal behaviors are permitted. The technique is designed to generate a large number of ideas by helping people to think creatively and allowing them to participate fully, without feeling inhibited or criticized by others.

breakdown

Identification of the smallest activities or tasks in a project for estimating, monitoring, and controlling purposes.

business risk

Risk—with its inherent potential for either profit or loss—that is associated with any particular endeavor.

chance

Possibility of an indicated outcome in an uncertain situation. *See also* probability.

closeout phase
Fourth phase in the generic project life cycle where all outstanding contractual issues are completed and documented in preparation for turning over the product or service to the customer.

coefficient of variation
The ratio of standard deviation to expected value. (See standard deviation and expected value.) A measure of relative uncertainty.

concept phase
First of four sequential phases in the generic project life cycle where the idea or notion for a project is first articulated. *Also called* idea, economic analysis, feasibility, *or* prefeasibility phase.

confidence interval
Limits of an uncertain quantity (like cost) between which there is a given probability of occurrence. Expressed as in "the n percent confidence interval." The confidence level is the left-hand lower confidence interval, so that one may say, "C is the nth confidence level," meaning there is an n percent probability of cost being between zero and C.

confidence level
Percentile. Used to indicate what certainty or faith is to be put into the sample being taken as representative of the entire population. The most common measure in the area is the confidence level for the mean.

consistent judgment matrix
A judgment matrix that expresses relationships like probabilities, so that if probability of I is m times that of J, and J is n times that of K, then the probability of I is mn times that of K. Since each entry is a ratio, r_{ij} of the probability of I divided by probability of J, then r_{ij} *times* r_{jk} *equals* r_{ik}.

contingency
(1) Provision for any project risk elements within the project scope; particularly important when comparison of estimates and actual data suggests that certain risk events are likely to occur. If an allowance for escalation is included in the contingency, such should be a separate item, calculated to fit expected price level escalation conditions for the project.
(2) Possible future action that may stem from presently known causes, the cost outcome of which cannot be determined accurately. *See also* reserve *and* contingency plan.

contingency plan

Plan that identifies alternative strategies to be used if specified risk events occur. Examples include a contingency reserve in the budget, alternative schedule activity sequences, and emergency responses to reduce the impacts of risk events.

contingency reserve

Quantity of money or time that is intended to reduce the impact of missed cost, schedule, or performance objectives, which can be only partly planned (sometimes called "known unknowns"), and that is normally included in the project's cost and schedule baseline.

contract work breakdown structure (CWBS)

Tool used to describe the total product and work to be done to satisfy a specific contract. Normally prepared by a contractor to reflect the statement of work in a specific contract or request for proposal. Used to define the level of reporting the contractor will provide the buyer. *See also* work breakdown structure.

control

(1) Process of comparing actual performance with planned performance, analyzing variances, evaluating alternatives, and taking corrective action as needed.

(2) One of the key risk response strategies, calling for reduction of the probability of a risk, reduction of the risk's impact, or deflection of the risk to another party. *Also called* mitigation.

cost baseline

Time-phased budget used to measure and monitor cost performance on the project. Developed by summing estimated costs by period and usually displayed in the form of an S-curve.

cost estimate

(1) Prediction of the expected monetary cost required to perform a task or acquire an item.

(2) Quantitative assessment of the likely costs of the resources required to complete project activities. May constitute a single value or a range of values and is based on understanding at a specific point in time.

cost estimating

Process of estimating the cost of the resources needed to complete project activities. Includes an economic evaluation, an assessment of project investment cost, and a forecast of future trends and costs.

cost estimating relationship (CER)
Mathematical relationship that defines cost as a function of one or more noncost parameters, such as performance, operating characteristics, or physical characteristics.

cost performance index (CPI)
Ratio of budgeted costs to actual costs (BCWP / ACWP). Often used to predict the amount of a possible cost overrun or underrun using the following formula: BAC ÷ CPI = EAC. *See also* earned value.

cost performance measurement baseline
Budget costs and measurable goals (particularly time and quantities) formulated for comparisons, analyses, and forecasts of future costs.

cost performance report (CPR)
Written account of cost and schedule progress and earned value, normally prepared monthly.

cost risk
(1) Risk associated with failing to complete tasks within the estimated budget allowances.
(2) Assessment of possible monetary loss or gain from the work to be done on a project.

critical path
In a project network diagram, the series of activities that determine the earliest completion of the project. Will change as activities are completed ahead of or behind schedule. Although normally calculated for the entire project, may also be determined for a milestone or subproject. Often defined as those activities with float less than or equal to a specified value, often zero. *See also* critical path method.

critical path method (CPM)
Network analysis technique used to predict project duration by analyzing the sequence of activities (path) that has the least amount of scheduling flexibility (the least amount of float). Early dates are calculated by a forward pass using a specified start date. Late dates are calculated by a backward pass starting from a specified completion date (usually the forward pass's calculated early finish date for the project).

critical risk
Risk that can jeopardize achievement of a project's cost, time, or performance objectives.

criticality index
The number of times an activity appears on the critical path during the simulation process.

cumulative density function (CDF)
A curve or mathematical expression that associates a probability to all values in the set of values over which it is defined so that the probability is that of the occurrence of a value less than or equal to a given value.

decision analysis
The examination of decision problems by analysis of the outcomes of decision alternatives, the probabilities of arrival at those outcomes, and the intervening decisions between selection of alternatives and arrival of outcomes. The attributes of the outcomes are examined and numerically matched against preference criteria.

decision making
Analyzing a problem to identify viable solutions and then making a choice among them.

decision tree
Diagram that shows key interactions among decisions and associated chance events as they are understood by the decision maker. Branches of the tree represent either decisions or chance events. The diagram provides for the consideration of the probability of each outcome.

deflection
Transference of all or part of a risk to another party, usually by means of a contract provision, insurance policy, or warranty.

Delphi technique
Form of participative expert judgment; an iterative, anonymous, interactive technique using survey methods to derive consensus on work estimates, approaches, and issues.

development phase
Second of four sequential phases in the generic project life cycle, where project planning and design typically occur. *Also called* planning phase.

earned value (EV)
Analysis of a project's schedule and financial progress as compared to the original plan.

estimate
Assessment of likely quantitative result, usually applied to project costs and durations. Should include some indication of accuracy (for example, ± X percent). Generally used with a modifier (such as preliminary, conceptual, or feasibility). Some disciplines use modifiers that imply specific accuracy ranges (such as order-of-magnitude, budget, and definitive, which have been traditionally used in engineering and construction projects), but are increasingly used in other industry applications.

expected monetary value (EMV)
Product of an event's probability of occurrence and the gain or loss that will result. For example, if there is a 50 percent probability of snow, and snow will result in a $100 loss, the expected monetary value of the snow is $50 (0.5 × $100).

expected time
Statistically calculated time estimate used in PERT estimating to determine the number of work periods an activity will consume. *See also* probabilistic estimating.

expert judgment
Opinions, advice, recommendations, or commentary proffered, usually upon request, by a person or persons recognized, either formally or informally, as having specialized knowledge or training in a specific area.

feasibility
Assessment of the capability for successful implementation; the possibility, probability, and suitability of accomplishment.

finish-to-finish (FF)
Relationship in a precedence diagramming method network in which one activity must end before the successor activity can end. *See also* logical relationship.

finish-to-start (FS)
Relationship in a precedence diagramming method network in which one activity must end before the successor activity can start. The most commonly used relationship in the precedence diagramming method. *See also* logical relationship.

float
Amount of time that an activity may be delayed from its early start without delaying the project end date. Derived by subtracting the early start from the late start or early finish from the late finish, and may change as the project progresses and as changes are made to the project plan. *Also called* slack, total float, *and* path float. *See also* free float.

free float
Amount of time that an activity may be delayed without delaying the early start of any immediately succeeding activities. *Also called* secondary float.

Gantt chart
Graphic display of schedule-related information. Generally, activities or other project elements are listed down the left side of the chart, dates are shown across the top, and activity durations are displayed against the x and y axes as date-placed horizontal bars. Named after its developer, Henry Gantt.

general and administrative (G&A) expense
Management, financial, or other expense incurred by or allocated to an organizational unit for the general management and administration of the organization as a whole.

Graphical Evaluation and Review Technique (GERT)
Network analysis technique that allows for conditional and probabilistic treatment of logical relationships (for example, some activities may not be performed).

histogram
Timeline chart that shows the use of a resource over time.

impact
Estimate of the effect that a risk will have on schedule, costs, product quality, safety, and performance.

impact analysis
Qualitative or quantitative assessment of the magnitude of loss or gain to be realized should a specific risk or opportunity event—or series of interdependent events—occur.

implementation phase
 Third of four sequential phases in the generic project life cycle where
 the project plan is executed, monitored, and controlled. *Also called*
 execution *or* operation phase.

incentive share ratio
 The ratio of government-to-contractor assumption of cost or savings
 related to contract target cost.

independence (also statistical independence)
 The relationship between two or more events when knowledge of the
 probability of occurrence of one does not alter the probability of
 another.

independent cost estimate
 (1) Estimate of project costs conducted by individuals outside the
 normal project management structure.
 (2) Estimate of anticipated project costs by the project team; used to
 compare the reasonableness of contractor proposals.

insurable risk
 Risk that can be covered by an insurance policy. *Also called* pure risk.

insurance
 (1) Premium paid to a person or organization to cover some or all of the
 cost of a risk impact. *See also* impact.
 (2) Protection against a risk of loss or harm.

internal rate of return (IRR)
 Annual rate of earnings on an investment. IRR equates the value of the
 cash returns with invested cash and considers the application of
 compound interest factors. The formula is as follows:

$$\sum_{}^{n} \frac{\text{Periodic cash flow}}{(1+i)^t} = \text{Investment amount}$$

 where i = internal rate of return, t = each time interval, n = total number
 of time intervals, and Σ is summation.

judgment matrix
 A square array of values such that all reciprocal entries are positive. For
 every entry in row i and column j, there is an entry in row j and
 column i.

lessons learned
Documented information, usually collected through meetings, discussions, or written reports, to show how both common and uncommon project events were addressed. This information can be used by other project managers as a reference for subsequent project efforts.

lessons learned review
Audit or evaluation conducted immediately upon project completion by the project team to learn from the successes and failures recently experienced. The results of the review are documented for use by project team members and other interested parties as a reference and guide for future project activities. *Also called* postproject evaluation and review.

life-cycle cost (LCC)
Broad view of project cost management that considers the effect of project decisions on the cost of using the project's product. Evaluation of all costs associated with the project life cycle, including acquiring, operating, supporting, and (if applicable) disposing of the items being acquired so decisions can be made among alternatives.

logical relationship
Dependency between two project activities or between a project activity and a milestone. The four types of logical relationships in the precedence diagramming method are (1) finish-to-start—the "from" activity must finish before the "to" activity can start, (2) finish-to-finish—the "from" activity must finish before the "to" activity can finish, (3) start-to-start—the "from" activity must start before the "to" activity can start, and (4) start-to-finish—the "from" activity must start before the "to" activity can finish. *Also called* link.

management reserve
Separately planned quantity of money or time intended to reduce the impact of missed cost, schedule, or performance objectives, which are impossible to plan for (sometimes called "unknown unknowns").

milestone
(1) Task, with a zero duration and requiring no resources, that is used to measure the progress of a project and signifies completion or start of a major deliverable.
(2) Identifiable point in a project or set of activities that represents a reporting requirement or completion of a large or important set of activities. *Also called* key event.

milestone schedule
Schedule consisting of key events or milestones (generally, critical accomplishments planned at time intervals throughout the project) and used to monitor overall project performance. May be either a network or bar chart and usually contains minimal detail at a highly summarized level. *Also called* key event schedule, master schedule *or* summary schedule.

minor risk
Risk event that does not cause significant problems, no matter what its probability.

mitigation
Risk response strategy that decreases risk by lowering the probability of a risk event's occurrence or reducing the effect of the risk should it occur. *See also* acceptance *and* avoidance.

mitigation strategy
Carefully organized steps taken to reduce or eliminate the probability of a risk's occurring or the impact of a risk on a project.

mode
The highest point on a probability density function. The point on the function at which the probability changes from increasing to decreasing.

model
Way to look at an item, generally by abstracting and simplifying it to make it understandable in a particular context.

modified Churchman-Ackoff method
A means of ordering events in terms of likelihood to occur.

moment
A function (called the expectation) of a probability law, often referred to as an "nth moment," where n is any number and denotes an exponent on the uncertain quantity. For example, if x is a discrete uncertain quantity, the third moment is the sum of all values of x^3 times the probability of each respective value of x.

Monte Carlo analysis
A technique in which outcomes of events are determined by selecting random numbers subject to defined probabilities. If the random number falls within the limits of an outcome's probability, that outcome is chosen. The process is done on an iterative basis to determine "statistical" likelihood.

most likely time
In PERT estimating, the most realistic number of work periods the activity will consume.

multiplicative cost elements
The value of cost elements derived by a multiplication of other cost elements.

net present value (NPV)
Financial calculation that takes into account the time values of a stream of income and expenditure at a given interest rate.

network
(1) Graphic depiction of the relationships of project work (activities or tasks). *See also* network diagram.
(2) Communication facility that connects end systems; interconnected series of points, nodes, or stations connected by communication channels; or assembly of equipment through which connections are made between data stations.

network analysis
Identification of early and late start and finish dates for uncompleted portions of project activities. *Also called* schedule analysis. *See also* critical path method, Program Evaluation and Review Technique, *and* Graphical Evaluation and Review Technique.

network-based scheduling
Process of determining logical relationships among WBS work packages, activities, and tasks and then arranging same to establish the shortest possible project duration. Examples of these techniques include PERT, CPM, and PDM.

node
Junction point joined to some or all of the other dependency lines in a network; an intersection of two or more lines or arrows. *See also* arrow diagramming method *and* precedence diagramming method.

nominal group technique

Specific structured process of team brainstorming and creative problem solving that draws on individual and group strengths but prevents domination by any one individual. Consists of five separate steps as follows: (1) silent generation—individual team members write responses to a problem statement in silence; (2) round robin—each team member recites his or her responses, which are written on a chart; (3) clarification—the group discusses the remarks; (4) selection and ranking—each team member selects and ranks in priority order the top 3 to 10 ideas collected; and (5) final selection and ranking—the facilitator tallies the results and prepares the group's ranked set of ideas.

odds

The ratio of probabilities of occurrence and nonoccurrence. For example, for a throw of a fair die the probability of getting a 4 is ⅙. The odds are 5 to 1.

opportunity assessment

Examination of the uncertainty associated with the possible occurrence of an event that is expected to have a positive impact on a project.

optimistic time

In PERT estimating, the minimum number of work periods the activity will consume.

parametric cost estimating

Estimating approach that uses a statistical relationship between historical data and other variables (for example, lines of code in software development) to calculate an estimate.

pessimistic duration

In PERT estimating, the maximum number of work periods the activity will consume. *Also called* pessimistic time.

precedence diagramming method (PDM)

Network diagramming technique in which activities are represented by boxes (or nodes) and linked by precedence relationship lines to show the sequence in which the activities are to be performed. The nodes are connected with arrows to show the dependencies. Four types of relationships are possible: finish-to-finish, finish-to-start, start-to-finish, and start-to-start. *Also called* activity-on-node (AON) *or* activity-on-arc.

present value
Value in current monetary units of work to be performed in the future. Determined by discounting the future price of the work by a rate commensurate with the interest rate on the funds for the period before payment is required.

probabilistic estimating
Method of estimating that generally uses three values to compute a statistically weighted estimate. *See also* Program Evaluation and Review Technique.

probability
(1) Likelihood of occurrence.
(2) Ratio of the number of chances that an event may or may not happen to the sum of the chances of both happening and not happening.

probability analysis
Risk quantification technique that entails specifying a probability distribution for each variable and then calculating values for situations in which any one or all of the variables are changed at the same time.

probability density function (PDF)
A probability expression in which the area under the function between defined limits of the values on which it is defined represents the probability of the values within those limits.

probability mass function (PMF)
A function assigning probability to each value of uncertain quantity having only discrete or discontinuous values.

Program Evaluation and Review Technique (PERT)
Event-oriented, probability-based network analysis technique used to estimate project duration when there is a high degree of uncertainty with the individual activity duration estimates. PERT applies the critical path method to a weighted average duration estimate. The formula is

$$\frac{O + 4(ML) + P}{6}$$

where O = optimistic time, ML = most likely time, and P = pessimistic time.

programmatic risk
The risks involved in obtaining and using applicable resources and activities that may be outside the project manager's control but that can affect the project's direction.

project risk
(1) Cumulative effect of the probability of uncertain occurrences that may positively or negatively affect project objectives.
(2) Degree of exposure to negative events and their probable consequences (opposite of opportunity). Characterized by three factors: risk event, risk probability, and amount at stake.

project risk management
That part of project management that includes the processes involved with identifying, analyzing, and responding to project risk; consists of risk identification, risk quantification, risk response development, and risk response control.

quality risk
Failure to complete tasks to the required level of technical or quality performance.

quantitative risk assessment
Numeric analysis of risk estimates including probability of occurrence to forecast the project's schedule and costs using probabilistic data and other identified uncertainties to determine likely outcomes.

range estimating
Applying probabilistic modeling to cost estimates as an adjunct to traditional estimating, not as a substitute for it. Includes identifying the mathematical probability of a cost overrun, amount of financial exposure, risks and opportunities ranked according to bottom-line importance, and contingency required for a given level of confidence. Can also be used in schedule estimating.

regression analysis
Determination of the values of constants in a mathematical expression that gives results that are the closest to the observed values associated with values of the data used in the expression. Regression analysis is a process by which the relationship between paired variables can be described mathematically using the tendency of jointly correlated random variables to approach their mean.

request for proposals (RFP)
Type of bid document used to solicit proposals from prospective contractors for products or services. Used when items or services are of a complex nature and assumes that negotiation will take place between the buyer and the contractor.

reserve
Money or time provided for in the project plan to mitigate cost, schedule, or performance risk. *See also* management reserve *and* contingency reserve.

resource leveling
(1) Practicing a form of network analysis in which scheduling decisions (start and finish dates) are driven by resource management issues (such as limited resource availability or changes in resource levels).
(2) Evening out the peaks and valleys of resource requirements so that a fixed amount of resources can be used over time.
(3) Ensuring that a resource is maximized but not used beyond its limitations.

risk
See project risk.

risk allowance
Time or money budgeted to cover uncertainties because of inaccuracies in deterministic estimates or the occurrence of risk events. *See also* contingency reserve *and* management reserve.

risk analysis
Analysis of the probability that certain undesirable and beneficial events will occur and their impact on attaining project objectives. *See also* risk assessment.

risk and opportunity assessment model (ROAM)
Specific technique developed by ESI International to quantify the identified risks and opportunities associated with a particular project to help decide whether the project should be undertaken.

risk appraisal
Work involved in identifying and assessing risk.

risk assessment
(1) Review, examination, and judgment to see whether the identified risks are acceptable according to proposed actions.
(2) Identification and quantification of project risks to ensure that they are understood and can be prioritized. *Also called* risk evaluation.

risk assumption
A conscious decision to accept the consequences of the occurrence of a risk.

risk avoidance
See avoidance.

risk budget
Cost and schedule allowance that is held in reserve and spent only if uncertainties or risks occur. A combination of contingency and management reserves.

risk control
The process of continually monitoring and correcting the condition of the project.

risk database
Database for risks associated with a project.

risk deflection
See deflection.

risk description
Documentation of the risk element to identify the boundaries of the risk.

risk drivers
The technical, programmatic, and supportability facets of risk.

risk evaluation
See risk assessment.

risk event
Discrete occurrence that may affect a project, positively or negatively. *See also* project risk.

risk event status

(1) Measure of importance of a risk event. Also referred to as criterion value or ranking.

(2) Probability and impact of a risk as of the data date.

risk exposure

(1) Impact value of a risk multiplied by its probability of occurring.

(2) Loss provision made for a risk; requires that a sufficient number of situations in which this risk could occur have been analyzed.

risk factor

Risk event, risk probability, or amount at stake.

risk handling

The last critical element in the risk management process. The action or inaction taken to address risk issues identified and evaluated in the risk assessment and risk analysis efforts.

risk identification

Determining the risk events that are likely to affect the project and classifying them according to their cause or source.

risk management

See project risk management.

risk management plan

Documentation of the procedures to be used to manage risk during the life of a project and the parties responsible for managing various areas of risk. Includes procedures for performing risk identification and quantification, planning risk response, implementing contingency plans, allocating reserves, and documenting results.

risk management strategy

Formal statement of how risk management will be implemented for a project, what resources will be used, and, if applicable, what roles subcontractors will play.

risk mitigation

See mitigation.

risk planning
Forcing organized purposeful thought to the subject of eliminating, minimizing, or containing the effects of undesirable occurrences. It allows for isolating and minimizing risk, eliminating risk wherever possible, developing alternative courses of action, and establishing time and money reserves to cover risks that cannot be avoided.

risk portfolio
Risk data assembled and collated for project management.

risk prioritizing
Filtering, grouping, and ranking risks following assessment.

risk probability
Assessment of the likelihood that a risk event will occur.

risk quantification
Evaluation of the probability of a risk event's occurring and of its effect.

risk rating scheme
An evaluation structure, based on agreed-to values denoting probability of occurrence and severity of the effect of failure, used to rank risks.

risk response control
Process of implementing risk strategies, documenting risk, and responding to changes in risk during the life of the project.

risk response development
Identification of specific actions to maximize the occurrence of opportunities and minimize the occurrence of specific risks in a project.

risk summary
Description of each risk factor, including its effect, ownership, and recommendations for response development.

risk symptom
Indirect manifestation of an actual risk event, such as poor morale serving as an early warning signal of an impending schedule delay or cost overruns on early activities pointing to poor estimating. *Also called* risk trigger.

risk trigger
See risk symptom.

schedule risk
Risk that jeopardizes completing the project according to the approved schedule.

schedule simulation
Use of the project network as a model of the project with the results used to quantify the risks of various schedule alternatives, project strategies, paths through the network, or individual activities. Most schedule simulations are based on some form of Monte Carlo analysis.

scope risks
Risks associated with scope or the need for "fixes" to achieve the required technical deliverables.

simulation
Technique used to emulate a process; usually conducted a number of times to understand the process better and to measure its outcomes under different policies.

skew
The asymmetry of a probability density function. The skew is to the side of the mode under which lies the greatest area.

slack
See float.

sources of risk
Categories of possible risk events that may affect the project positively or negatively. Descriptions of risk sources should include rough estimates of the probability that a risk event from that source will occur, the range of possible outcomes, the expected timing, and the anticipated frequency of risk events from the source.

standard deviation
The square root of the variance. Often used because it is expressed in the same units as the random variable itself and can be depicted on the same axes as the probability density function of which it is a character-istic.

start-to-finish
Relationship in a precedence diagramming method network in which one activity must start before the successor activity can finish.

start-to-start
Relationship in a precedence diagramming method network in which one activity must start before the successor activity can start.

statement of work (SOW)
Narrative description of products or services to be supplied under contract that states the specifications or other minimum requirements; quantities; performance dates, times, and locations, if applicable; and quality requirements. Serves as the basis for the contractor's response and as a baseline against which the progress and subsequent contractual changes are measured during contract performance.

supportability risk
The risks associated with fielding and maintaining systems that are being developed or have been developed and are being deployed.

task
Well-defined component of project work; a discrete work item. There are usually multiple tasks for one activity. *See also* activity.

technical risk
The risk associated with developing a new design to provide a greater level of performance than previously demonstrated or to accommodate new constraints, such as size or weight.

templates
Set of guidelines that provides sample outlines, forms, checklists, and other documents.

total float (TF)
See float.

unacceptable risk
Exposure to risks that are significant enough to jeopardize an organization's strategy, present dangers to human lives, or represent a significant financial exposure, such that avoidance or mitigation is imperative.

uncertainty
(1) Situation in which only part of the information needed for decision making is available.
(2) Lack of knowledge of future events.

value analysis

Activity concerned with optimizing cost performance. Systematic use of techniques to identify the required functions of an item, establish values for those functions, and provide the functions at the lowest overall cost without loss of performance.

variance

Actual or potential deviation from an intended or budgeted amount or plan. Difference between a plan and actual time, cost, or performance.

WBS dictionary

Collection of work package descriptions that includes, among other things, planning information such as schedule dates, cost budgets, and staff assignments.

work breakdown structure (WBS)

Deliverable-oriented grouping of project elements that organizes and defines the total scope of the project. Each descending level is an increasingly detailed definition of a project component. Project components may be products or services. *See also* contract work breakdown structure.

workaround

Unplanned response to a negative risk event. Distinguished from contingency plan because it is not planned in advance of the occurrence of the risk event.

BIBLIOGRAPHY

Air Force Systems Command (AFSC). "Air Force Systems Command Software Risk Management." AFSCP800-XX (Draft). June 1987.

———. "Software Reporting Metrics." Hanscom Air Force Base, Mass.: Electronic Systems Division, November 1985.

American Heritage Dictionary of the English Language, 3rd ed. Boston: Houghton Mifflin, 1992.

Atzinger, E.M., et al. *Compendium on Risk Analysis Techniques.* AD 746245, LD 28463. Aberdeen Proving Ground, Md.: DARCOM Material Systems Analysis Activity, 1972.

Baird, Bruce. *Managerial Decisions Under Uncertainty.* New York: John Wiley & Sons, Inc., 1989.

Bernstein, Peter L. *Against the Gods.* New York: John Wiley & Sons, Inc., 1996.

Boehm, Barry. *Software Risk Management.* Washington, D.C.: IEEE Computer Society Press, 1989.

Carter, Bruce, et al. *Introducing RISKMAN Methodology.* Oxford, England: NCC Blackwell, 1994.

Caver, T.V. "Risk Management As a Means of Direction and Control." *Fact Sheet Program Managers Notebook.* Fort Belvoir, Va.: Defense Systems Management College, April 1985.

Defense Systems Management College (DSMC). *DSMC Systems Engineering Management Guide.* Ft. Belvoir, Va.: Defense Systems Management College, 1990.

———. "Integrated Logistics Support." Ft. Belvoir, Va.: Defense Systems Management College, October 1985.

————. *Risk Management: Concepts and Guidance*. Ft. Belvoir, Va.: Defense Systems Management College, 1986.

Government Accounting Office. "Technical Risk Assessment—The Status of Current DOD Efforts." Washington, D.C.: General Accounting Office, April 1986.

Kipp, Jonathan D., and Murrey E. Loflin. *Emergency Incident Risk Management: A Safety and Health Perspective*. New York: Van Nostrand Reinhold, 1996.

Megill, Robert E. *An Introduction to Risk Analysis*. Tulsa, Okla.: PennWell Publishing Company, 1984.

Meredith, Jack R., and Samuel J. Mantel, Jr. *Project Management: A Managerial Approach*. New York: John Wiley & Sons, Inc., 1995.

Modarres, M. *What Every Engineer Should Know About Reliability and Risk Analysis*. New York: Marcel Dekker, Inc., 1993.

Pfaffenberger, Roger C., and James H. Patterson. *Statistical Methods for Business and Economics*. Homewood, Ill.: Irwin, 1977.

Project Management Institute Standards Committee. *A Guide to the Project Management Body of Knowledge*. Upper Darby, Pa.: Project Management Institute, 1996.

Winkler, R.L. "The Quantification of Judgment: Some Methodological Suggestions." *Journal of the American Statistical Association* 62 (1967): 1105–1120.

INDEX

ALSO FROM ESI INTERNATIONAL

PMP Challenge!, J. LeRoy Ward and Ginger Levin, D.P.A. 1996. 480 pages. Spiral-bound. $44.95.

Quiz yourself on your knowledge of the PMBOK, specifically, and project management, in general, with this flash card study aid containing 480 thought-provoking questions. This publication addresses the topics you need to know to pass the PMP certification exam and will improve your chances of passing it the first time around.

PMP Exam: Practice Test and Study Guide, Editor, J. LeRoy Ward. 1997. 218 pages. Spiral-bound. $29.95.

Are you looking for a rigorous practice test that will provide an excellent representation of the types of questions you are sure to find on the PMP certification exam? This publication contains 320 multiple-choice questions (40 per PMBOK area)—including questions on the new project integration management area—and provides a rationale and a reference with each correct answer.

Project Management Terms: A Working Glossary, Editor, J. LeRoy Ward. 1997. 181 pages. Softcover. $29.95.

This practical pocket-size glossary was developed *by* project managers *for* project managers—and all those with whom they interact. It contains more than 1,600 terms, phrases, and acronyms. Each entry is succinctly defined and cross referenced. Users will find it an indispensable tool in communicating effectively in the global world of project management.

World-Class Contracting: 100+ Best Practices for Building Successful Business Relationships, Gregory A. Garrett. 1997. Hardcover. 301 pages. $59.95.

Here is a comprehensive process approach to contract management from both the buyer's *and* the seller's perspectives. It is a hard-hitting, usable guide supplemented with numerous process diagrams, best practices and lessons learned from leading multinational organizations, sample forms, tools, and techniques that the practitioner will find relevant and valuable.

To order one of the books, call 1-703-558-3020 or visit our Web site at http://www.esi-intl.com.

Knowledge & Skills Assessment, ESI International. 1996.

Identify individual and organizational levels of knowledge and skill relative to the nine sections of the PMBOK using this self-scoring tool. Individuals answer multiple-choice questions to determine the areas in which they require the most improvement. Organizations often use the composite results from groups to determine what their educational and training priorities should be.

Project Management Competencies, ESI International in association with The Clark Wilson Group. 1995.

Use this invaluable assessment tool to reliably measure 21 critical traits of an effective project manager. It is the only sound means of sizing up a person's potential for project management or enabling current project managers to determine precisely how they must change to experience greater success. Each scale has been validated, and the instrument is machine scorable.

To find out more about these instruments, call 1-703-558-3020.